THE OFFICIAL COLORING BOOK

T0025912

THE OFFICIAL COLORING BOOK

ISBN: 9781803368054

Published by
Titan Books
A division of Titan Publishing Group Ltd
144 Southwark Street
London
SE1 0UP
www.titanbooks.com

First edition March 2024
2 4 6 8 10 9 7 5 3

Comic illustrations throughout by Arthur Adams, Matt Frank, Tadd Galusha,
Simon Gane, Zach Howard, John Kantz, Eric Powell, James Stokoe and Jeff Zornow

Illustrations on pages 6, 14, 20, 21, 25, 42, 45, 58-59 and 62 by Álvaro Sarraseca
Illustrations on pages 8, 10, 16, 18, 31, 34, 38, 49 and 56 by David Cabeza

Did you enjoy this book? We love to hear from our readers.
Please e-mail us at: readerfeedback@titanemail.com
or write to Reader Feedback at the above address.

To receive advance information, news, competitions, and exclusive offers online, please sign up
for the Titan newsletter on our website: www.titanbooks.com

A CIP catalogue record for this title is available from the British Library.

Printed and bound in the United Kingdom

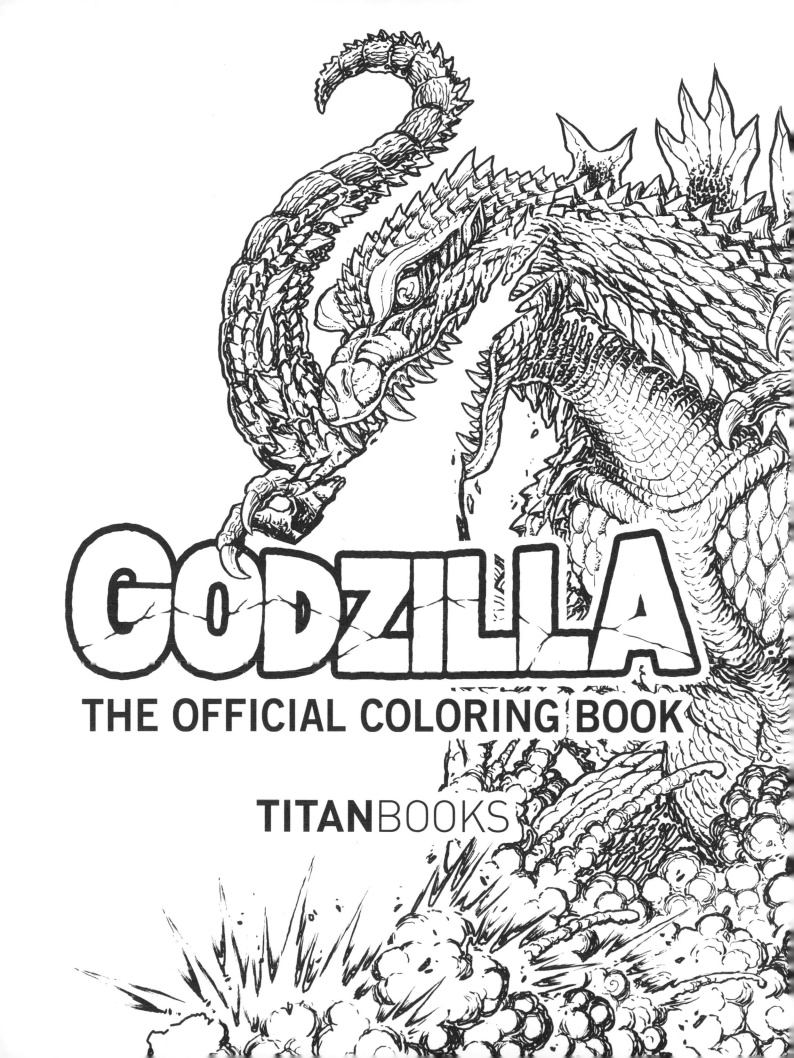

GODZILLA

THE OFFICIAL COLORING BOOK

TITANBOOKS

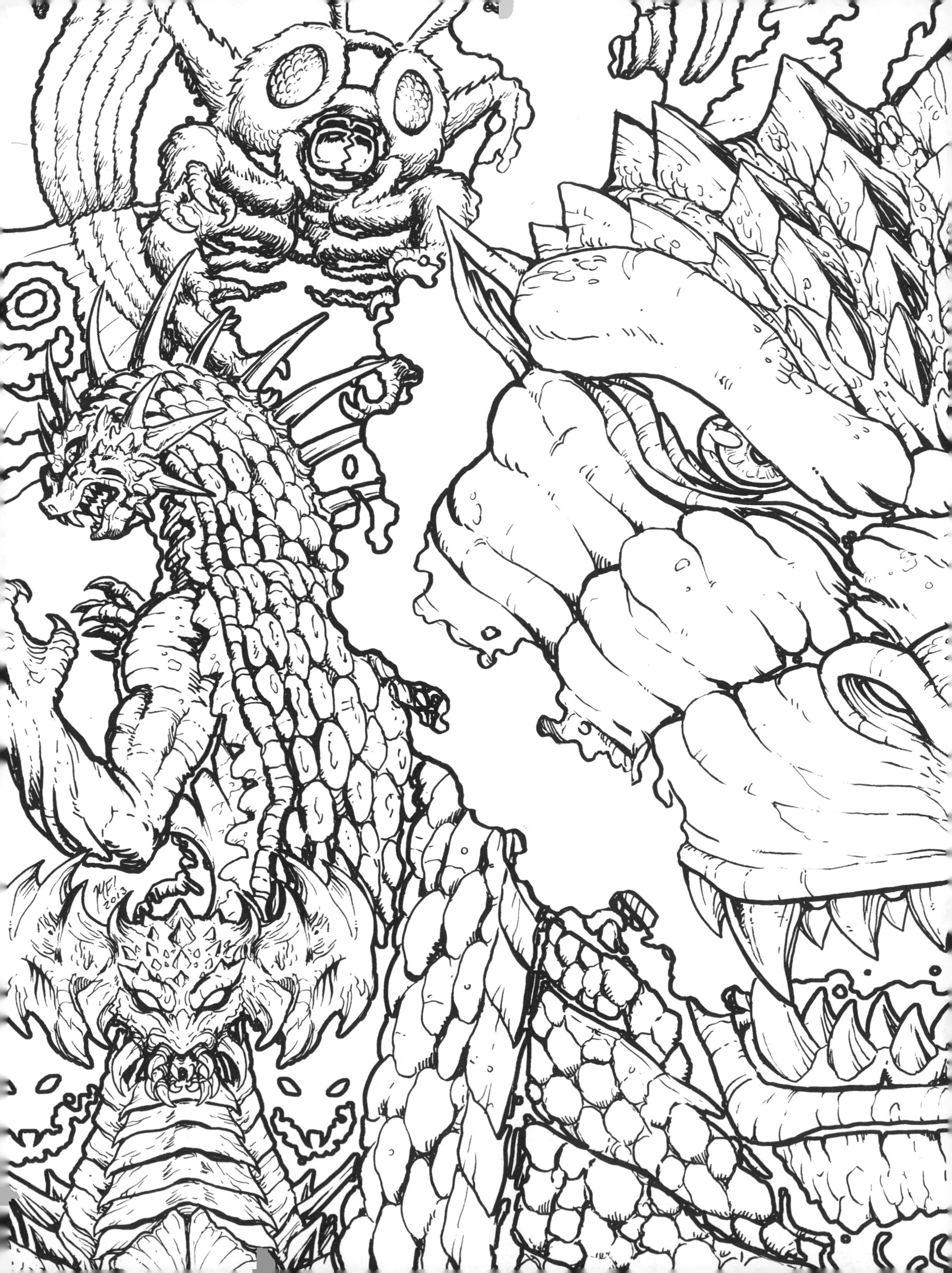

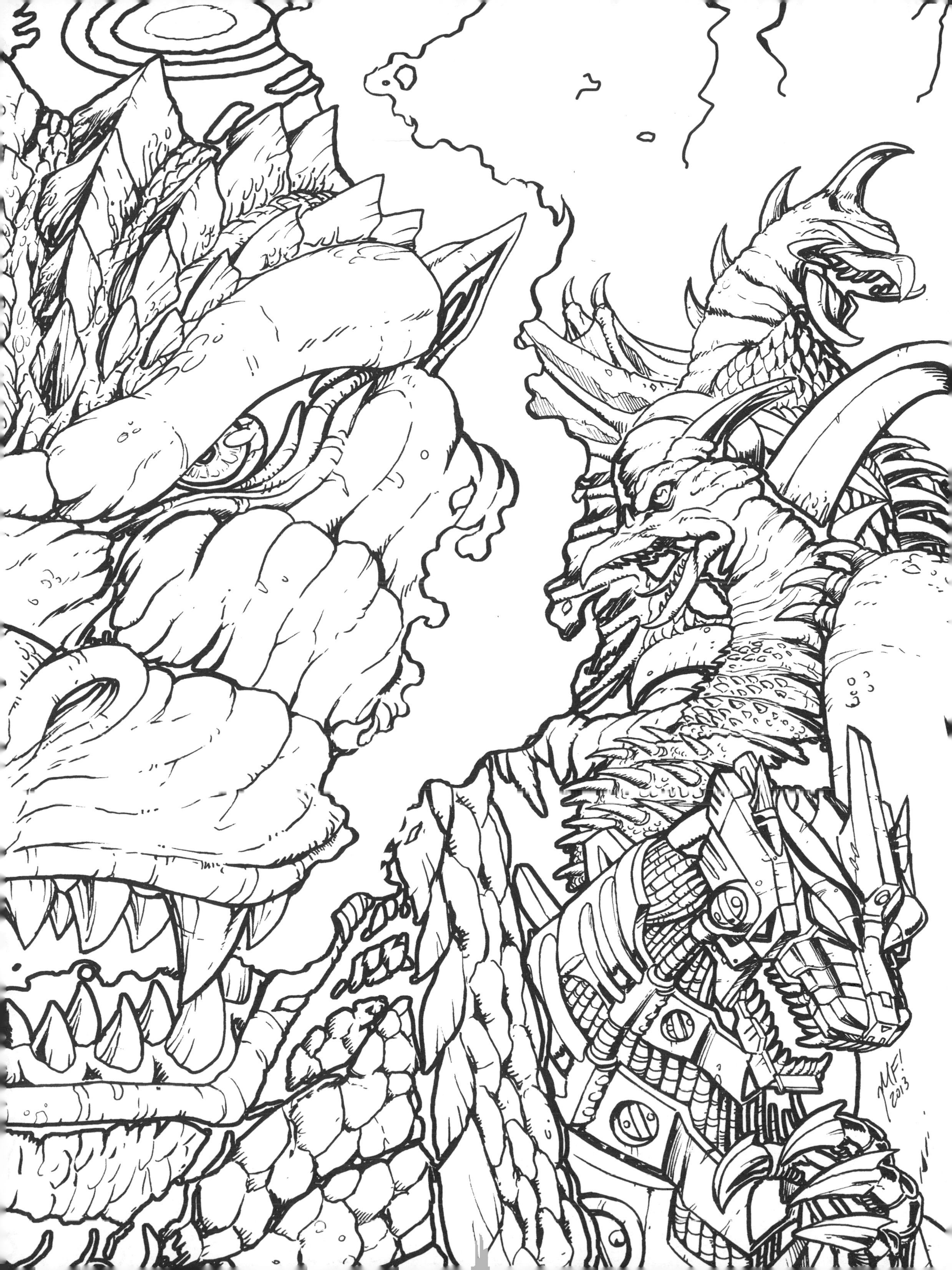
MF!
2013

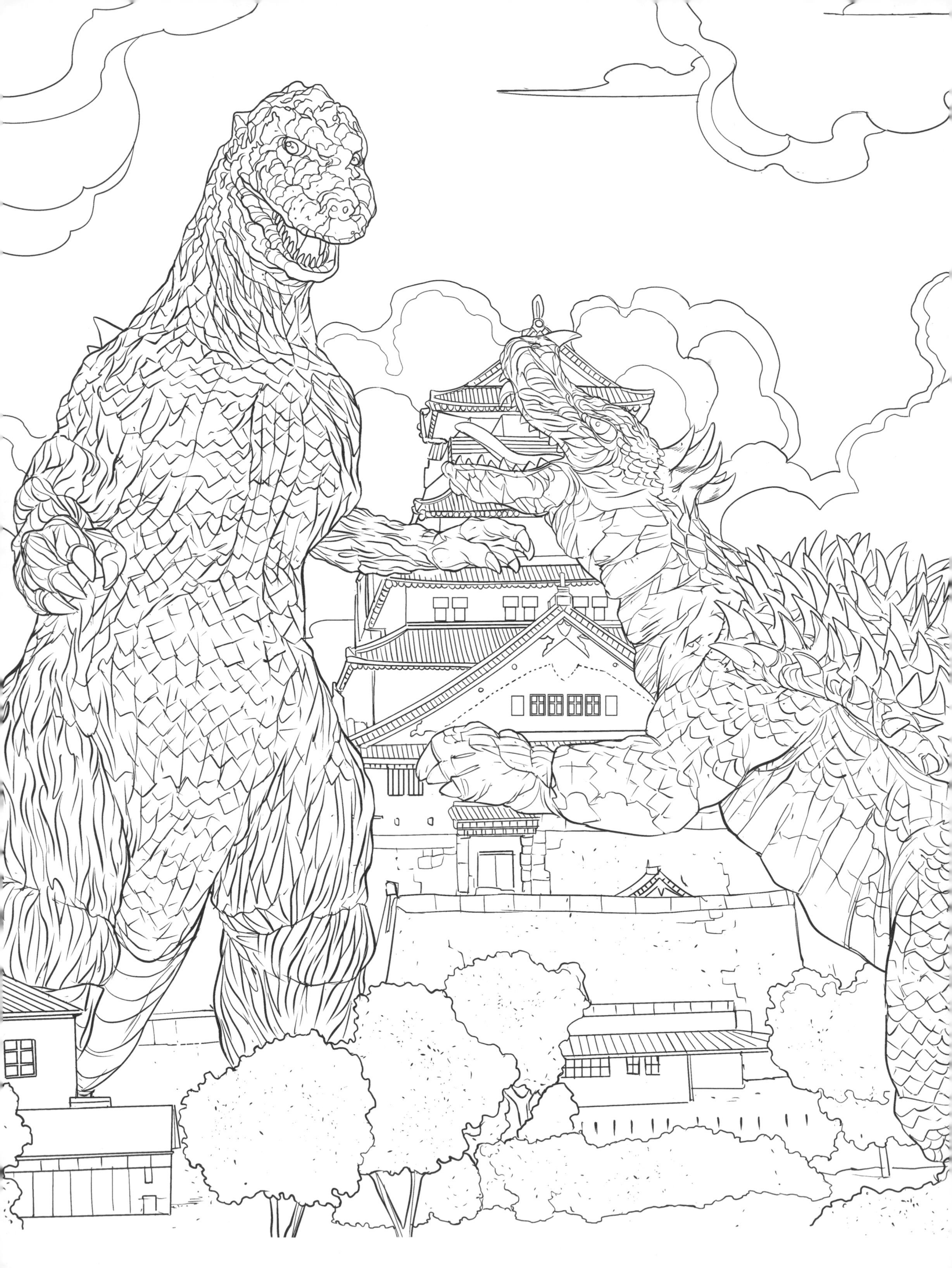

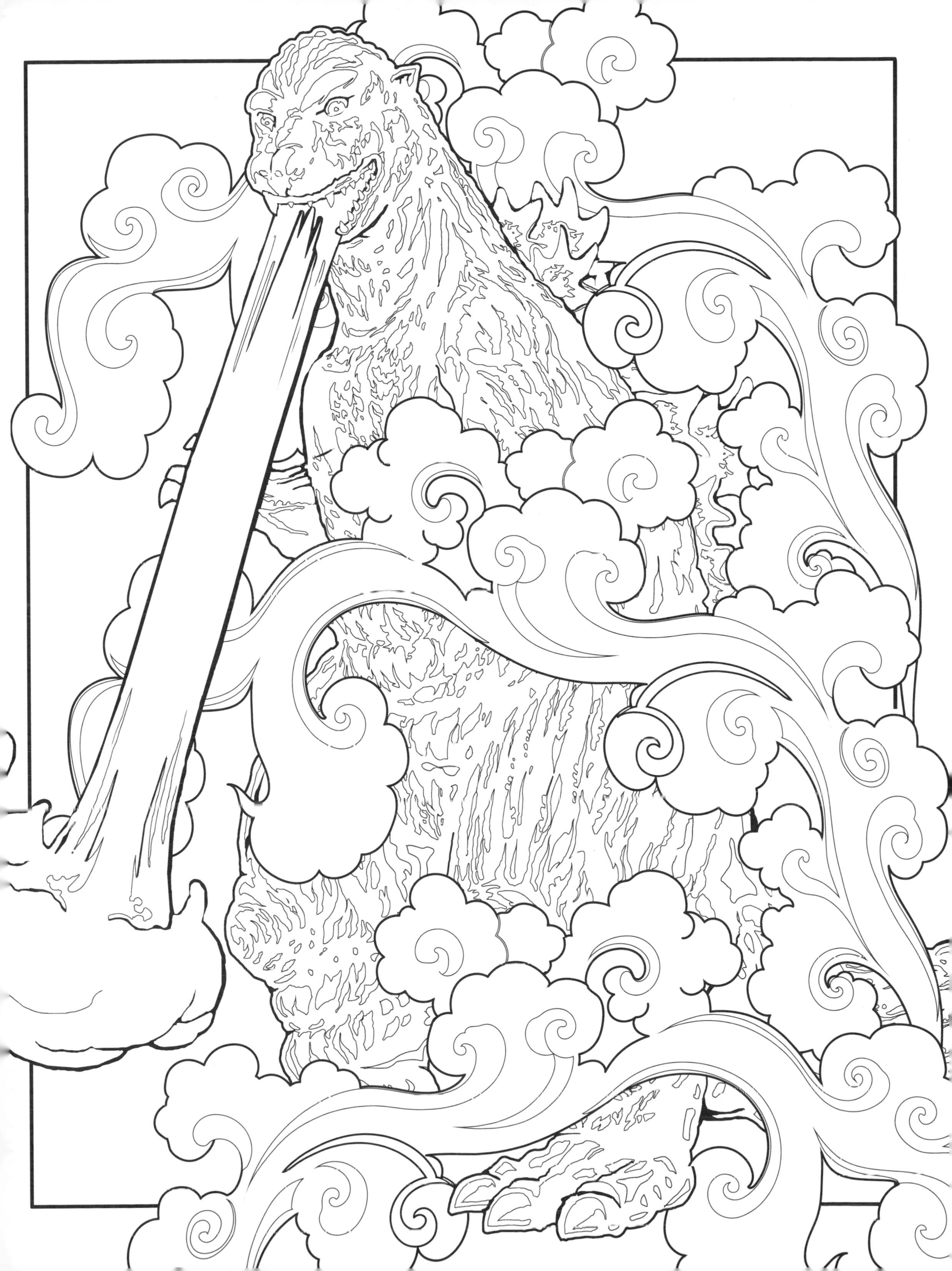

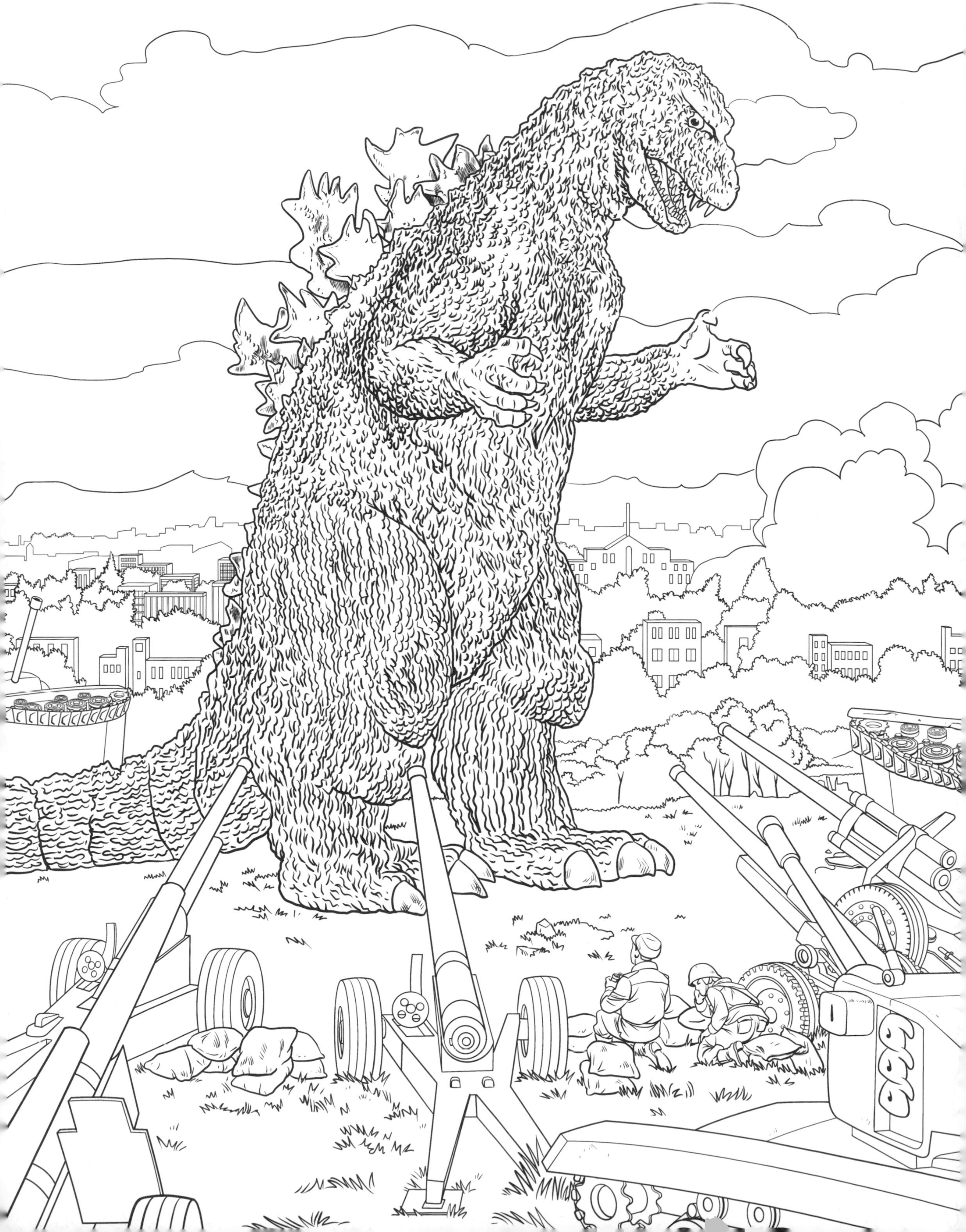

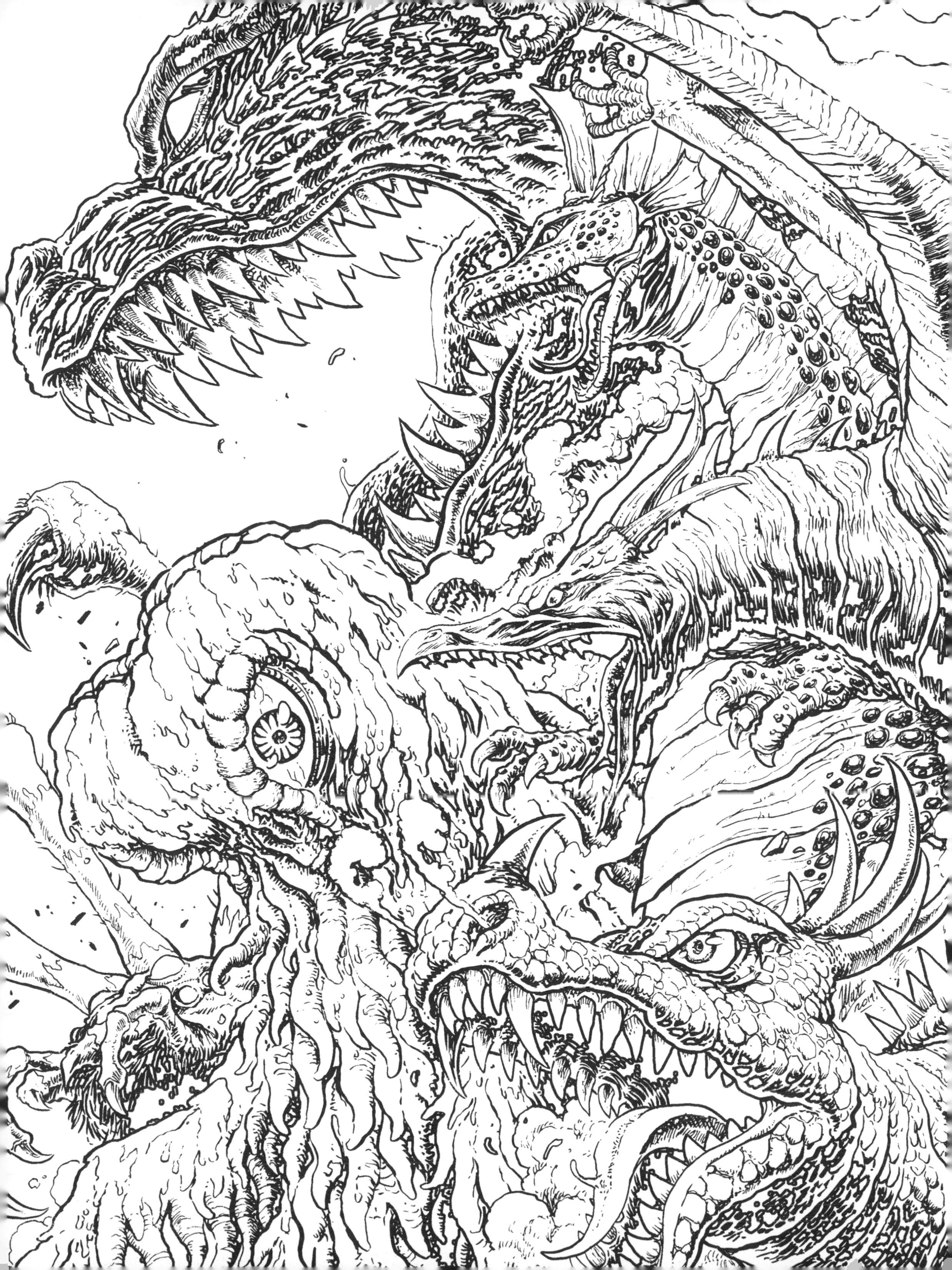

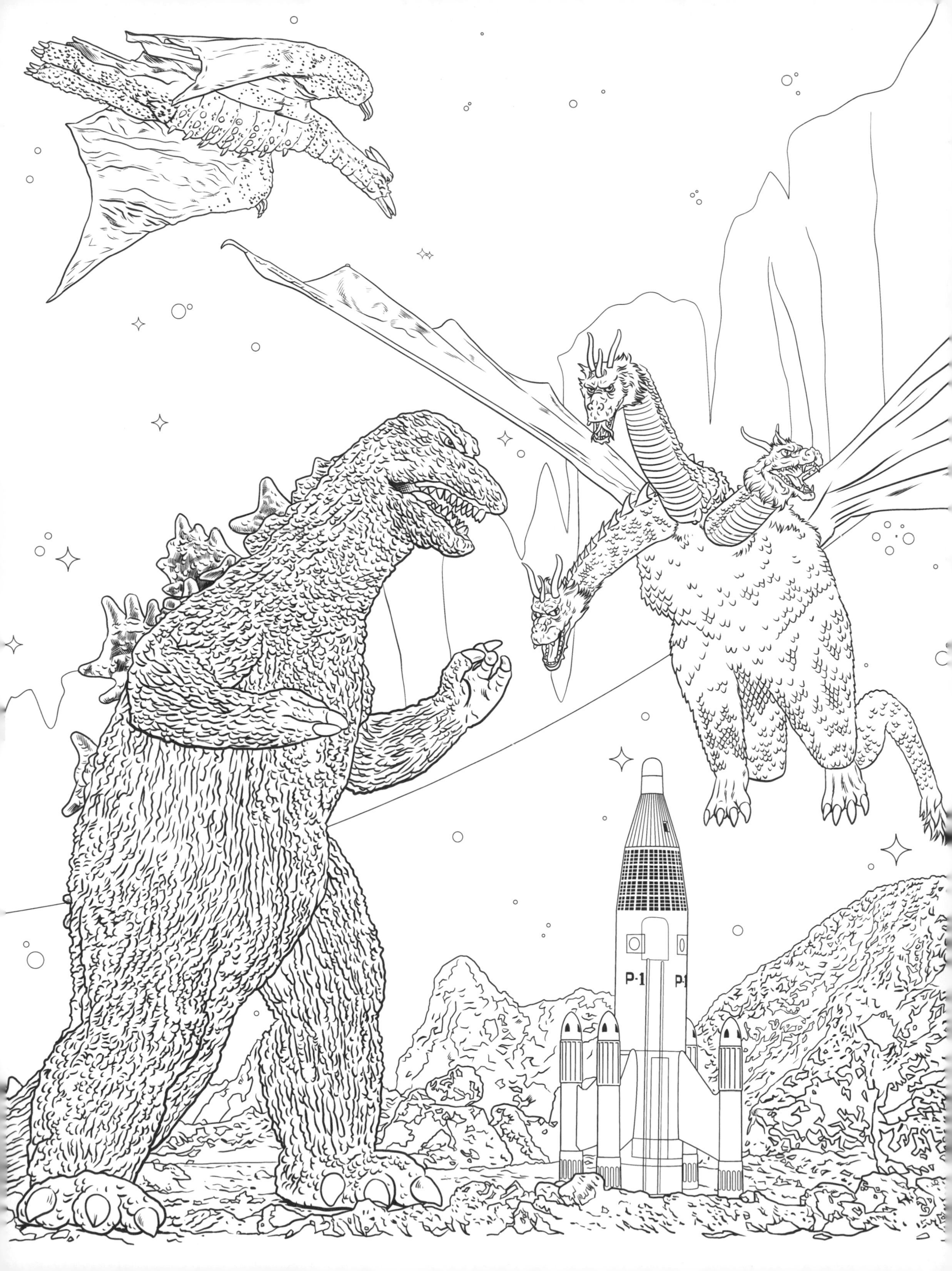
P-1
P-1

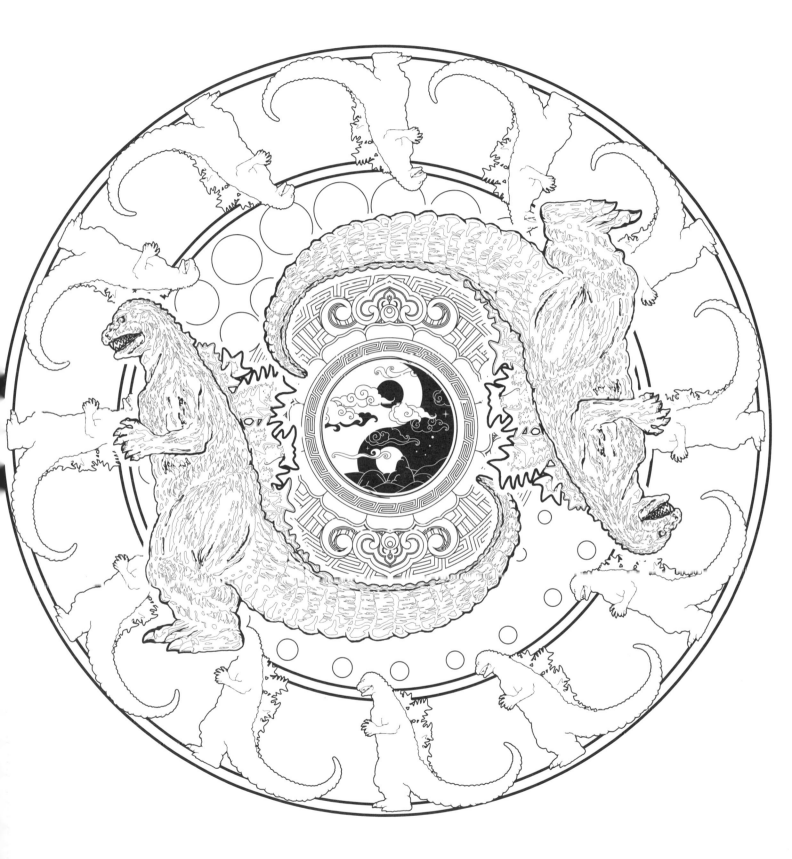

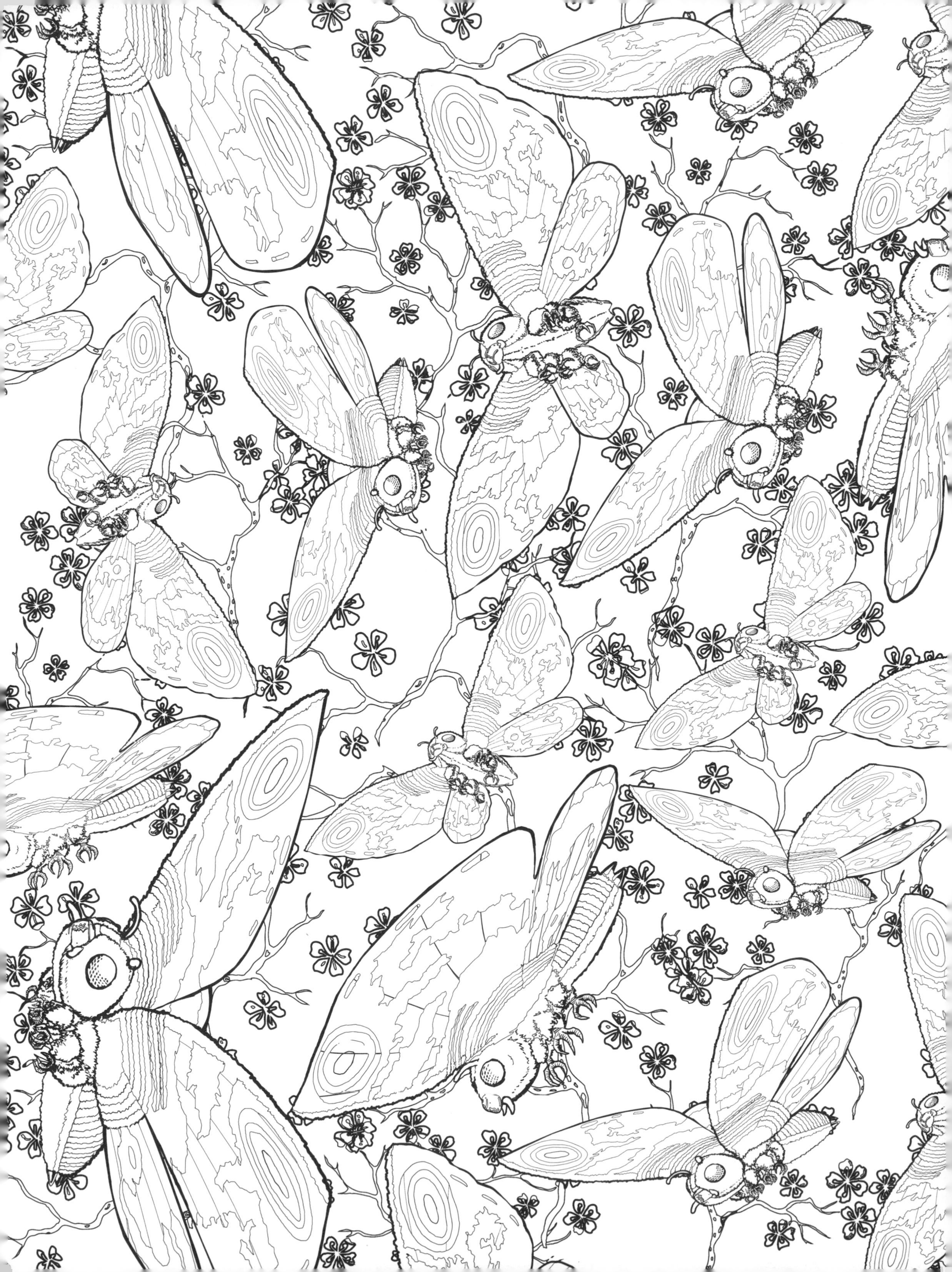

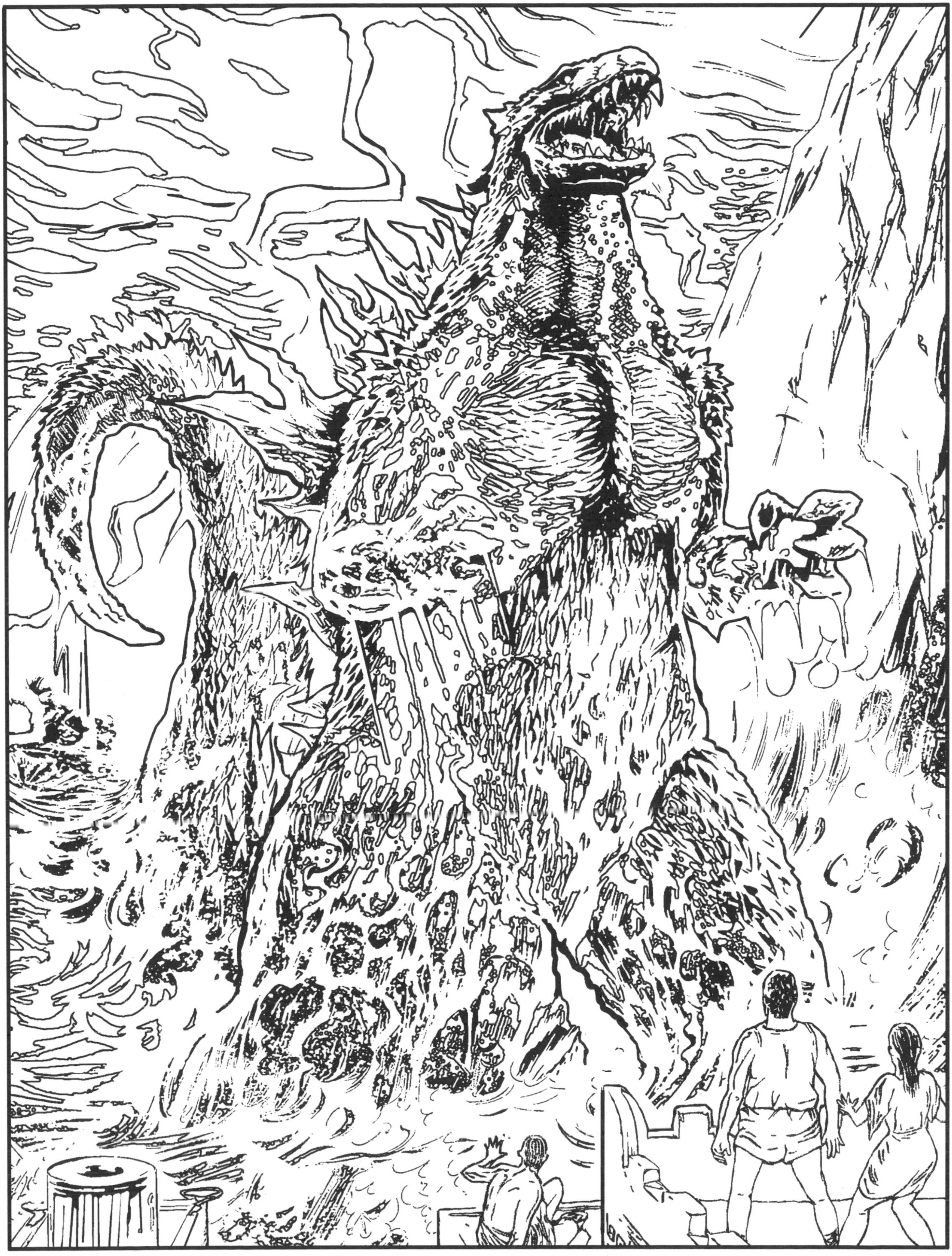

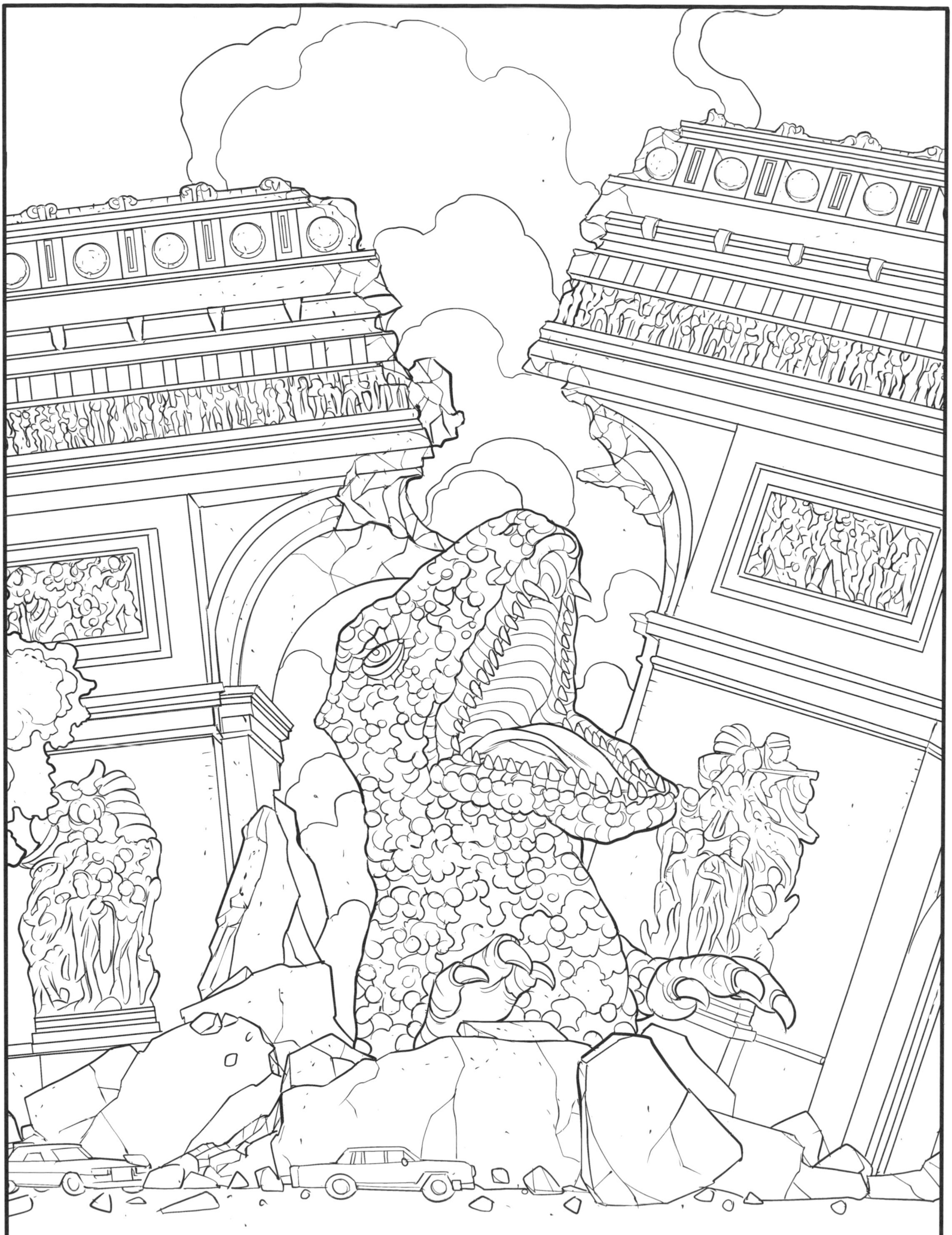

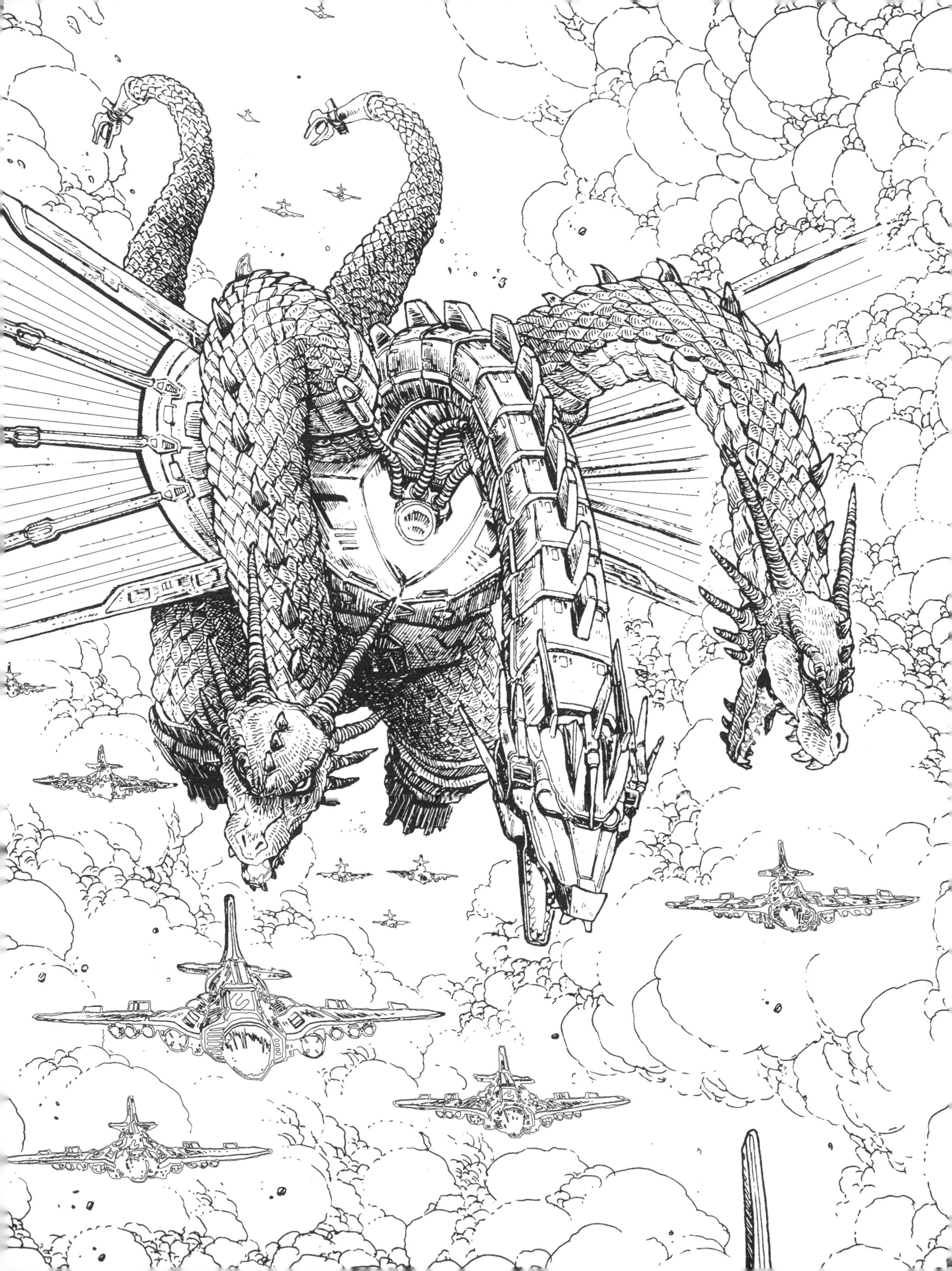

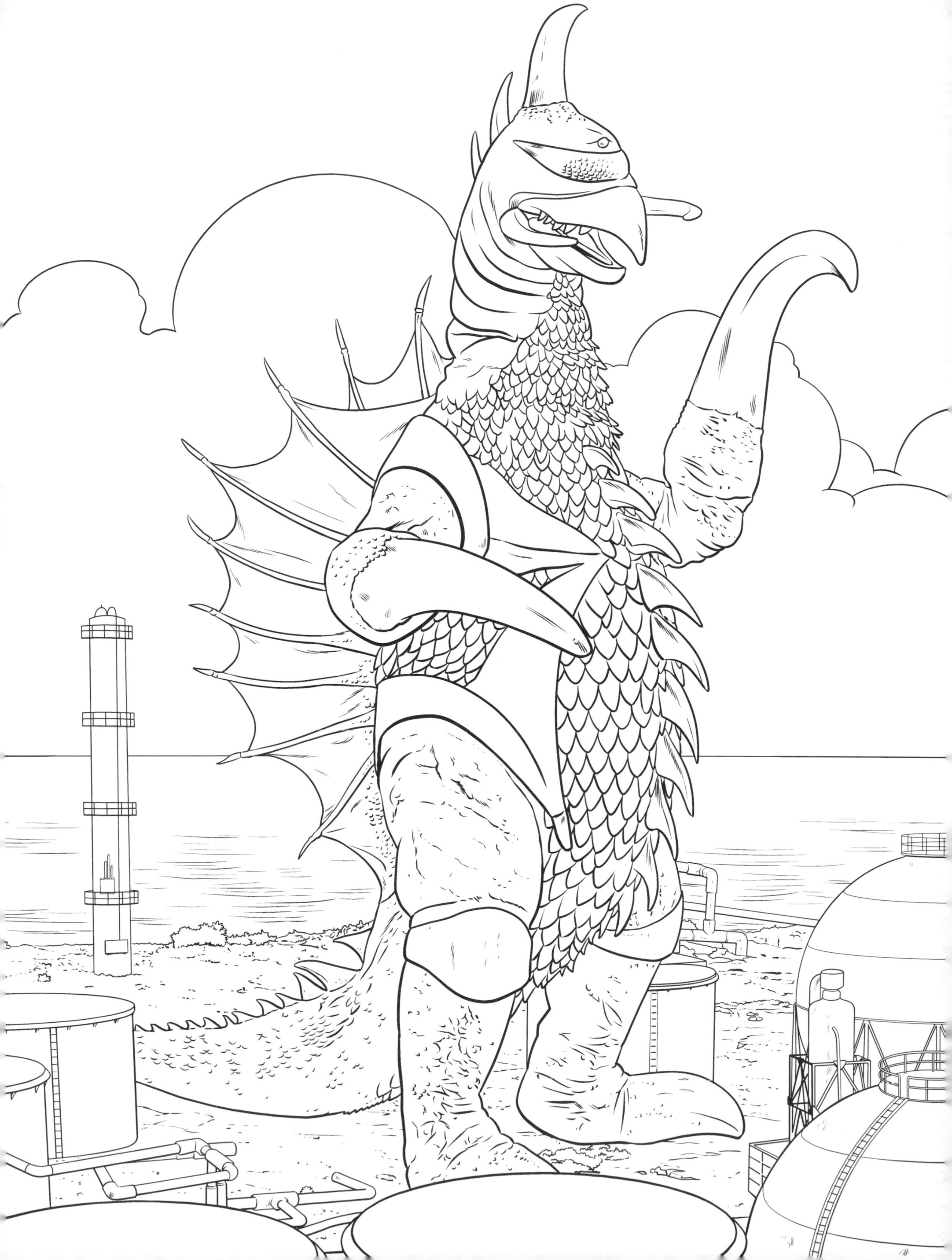

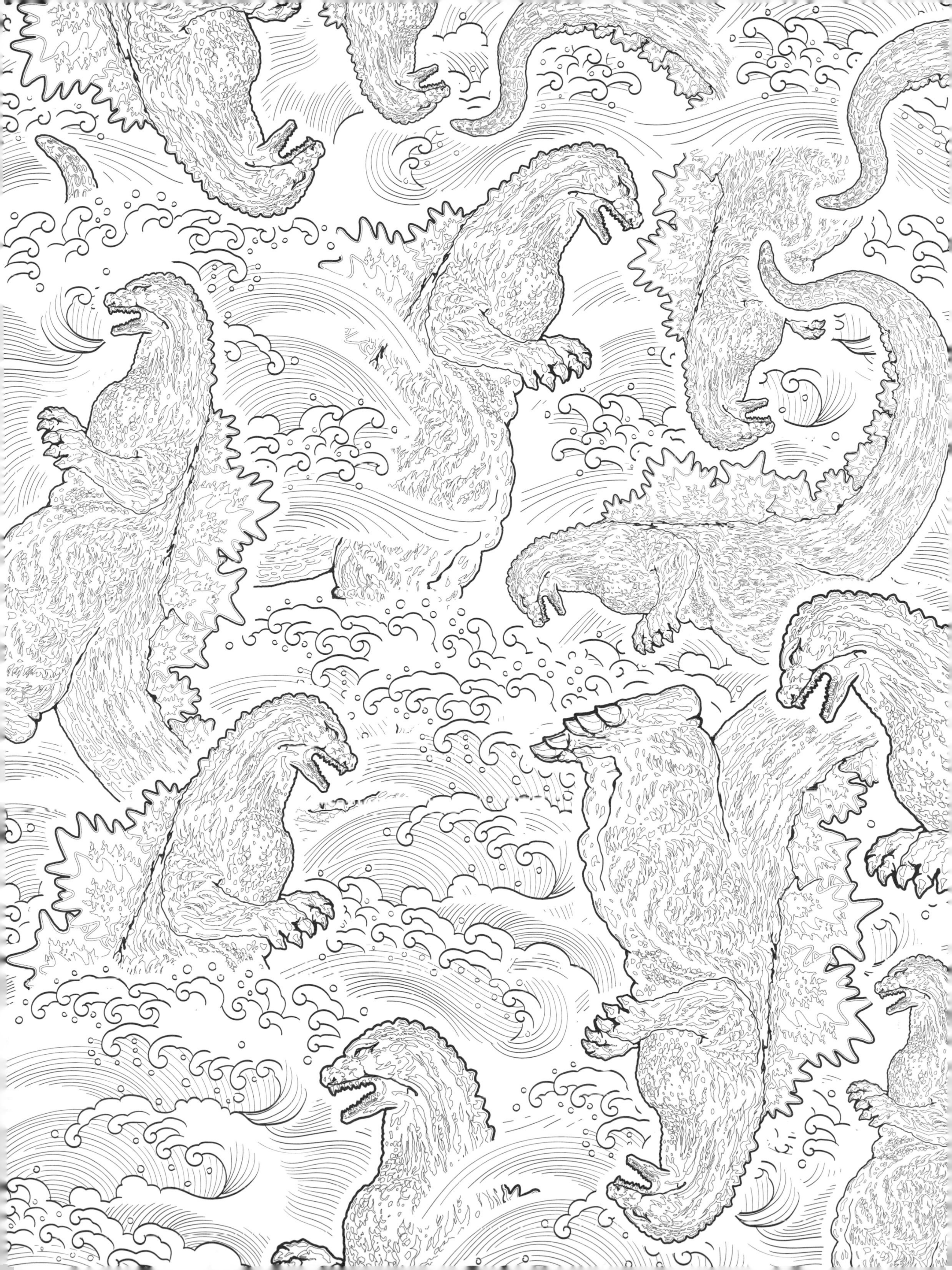

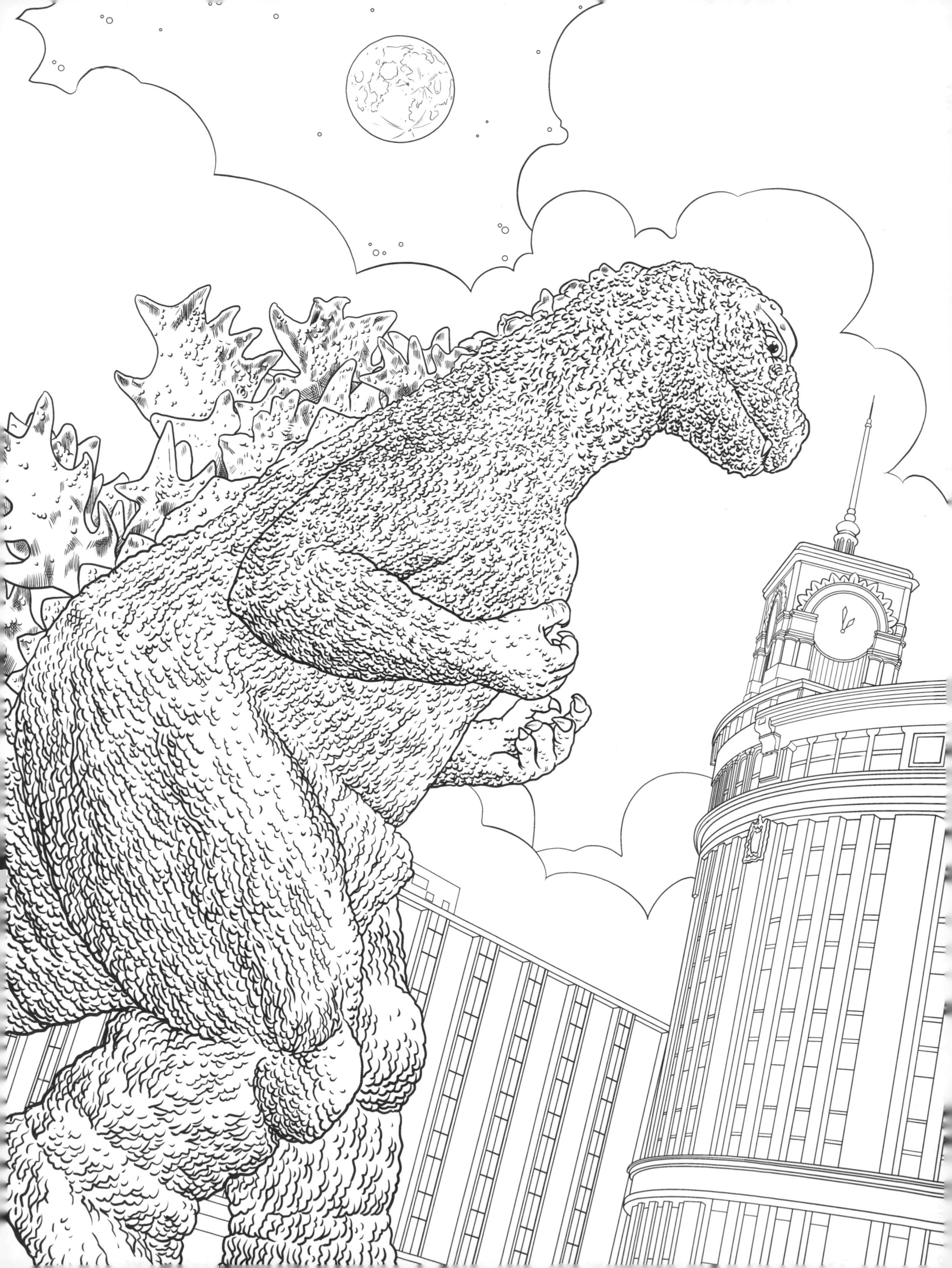

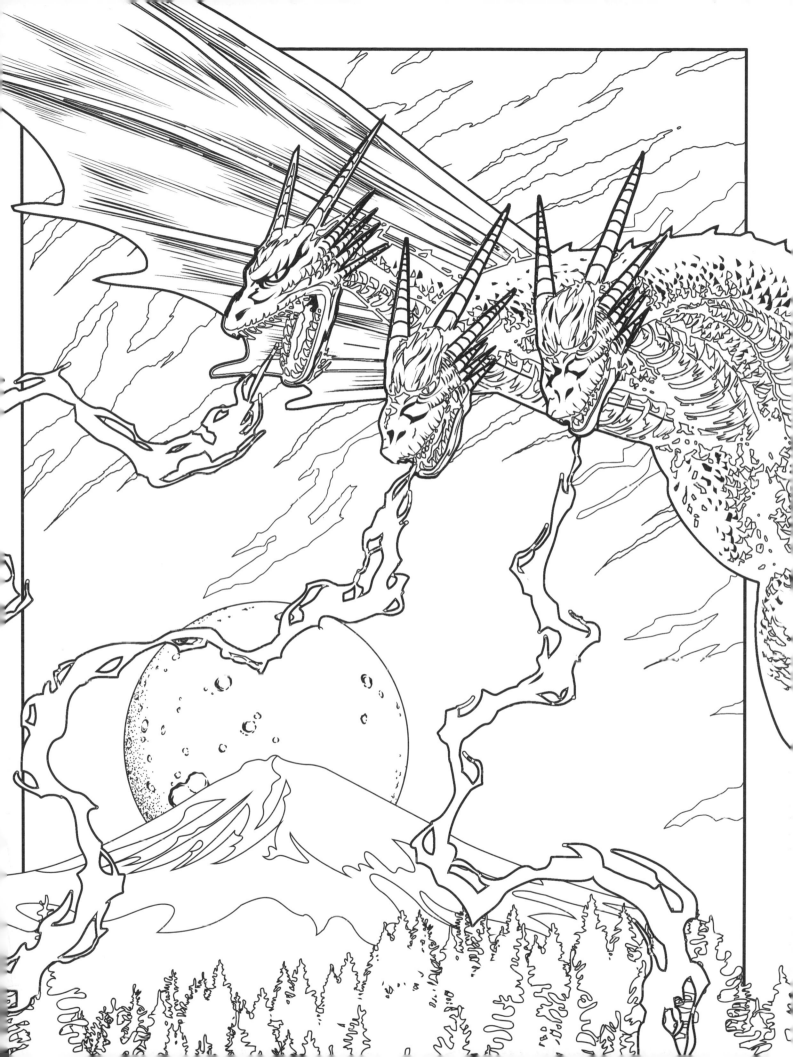

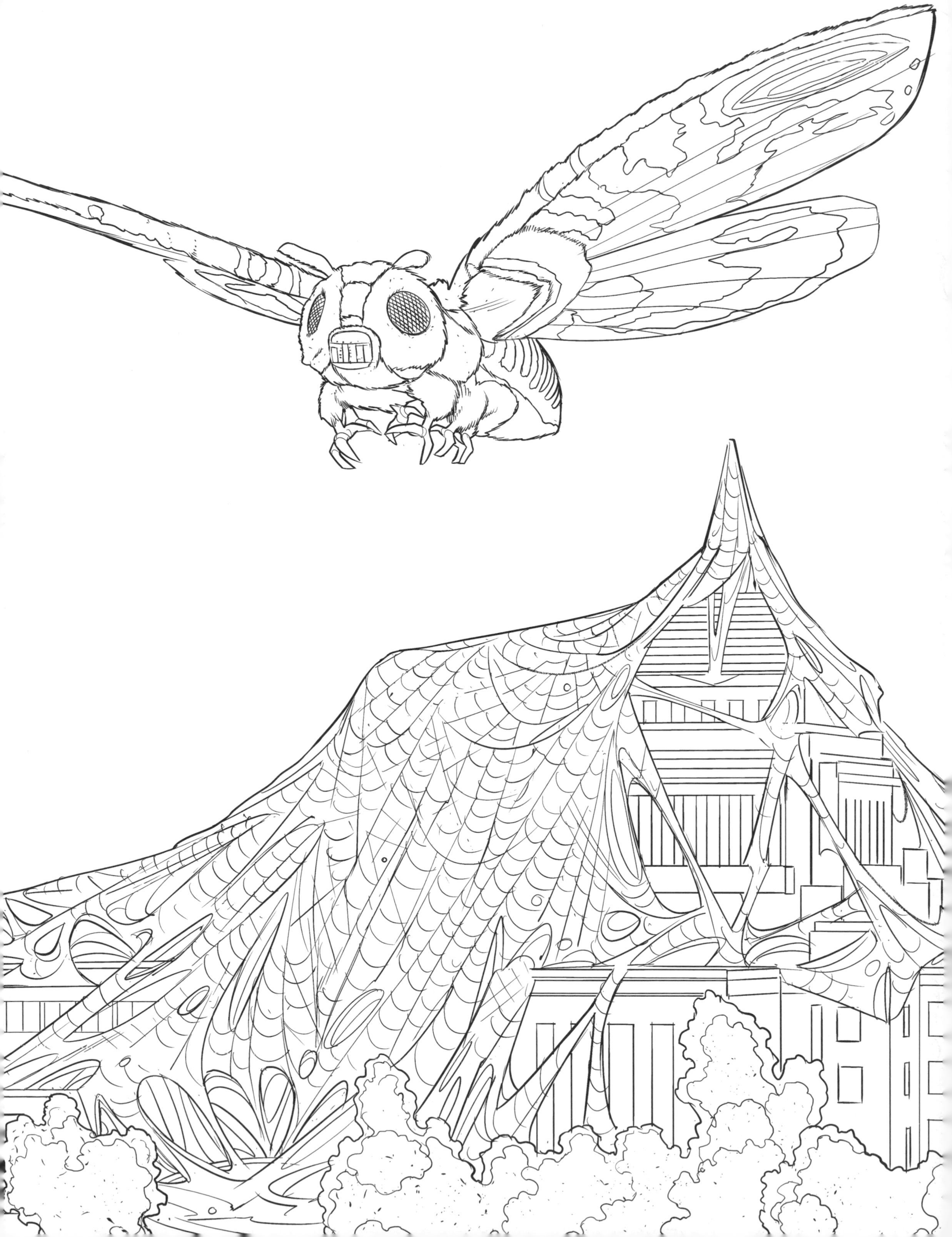

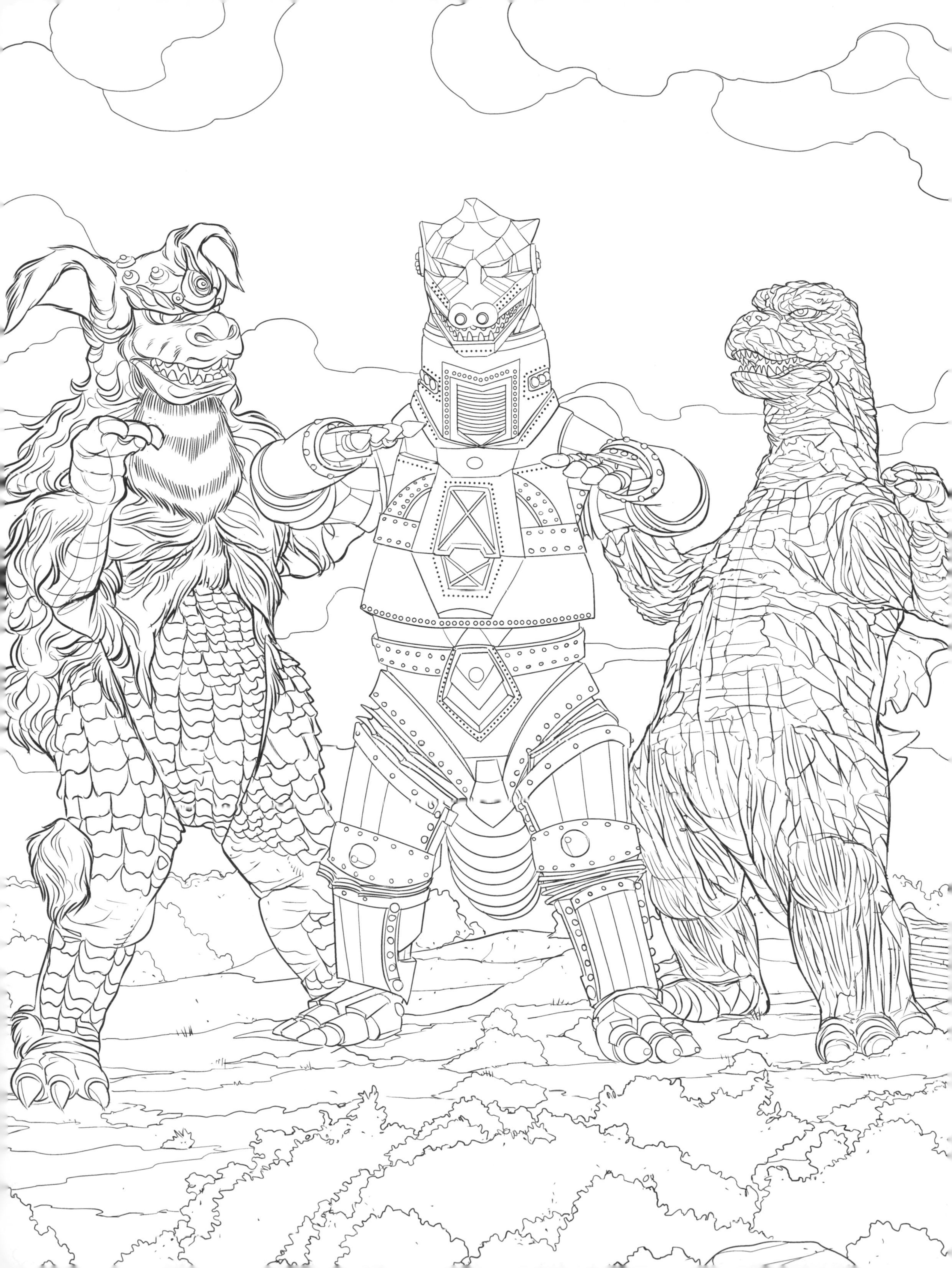

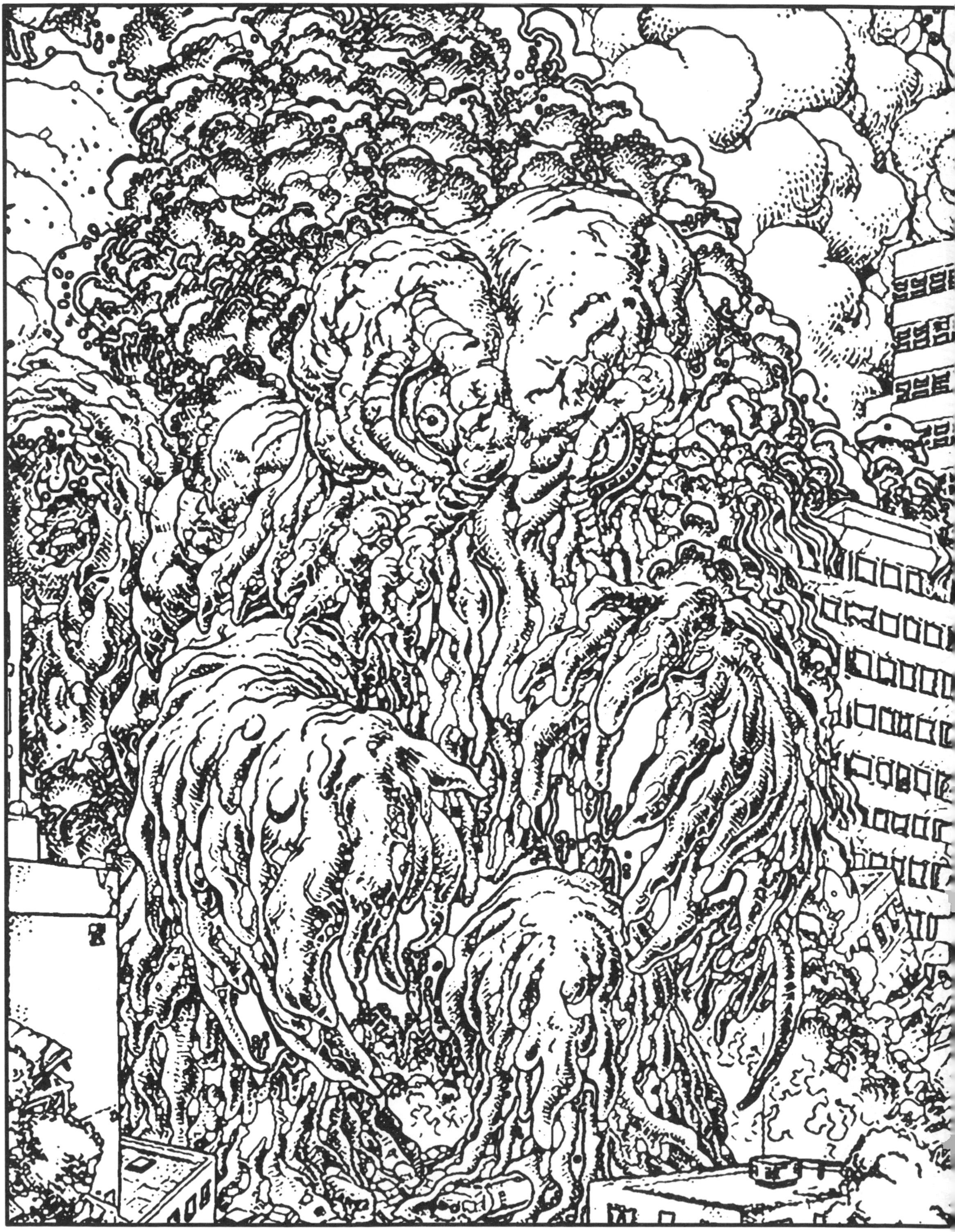

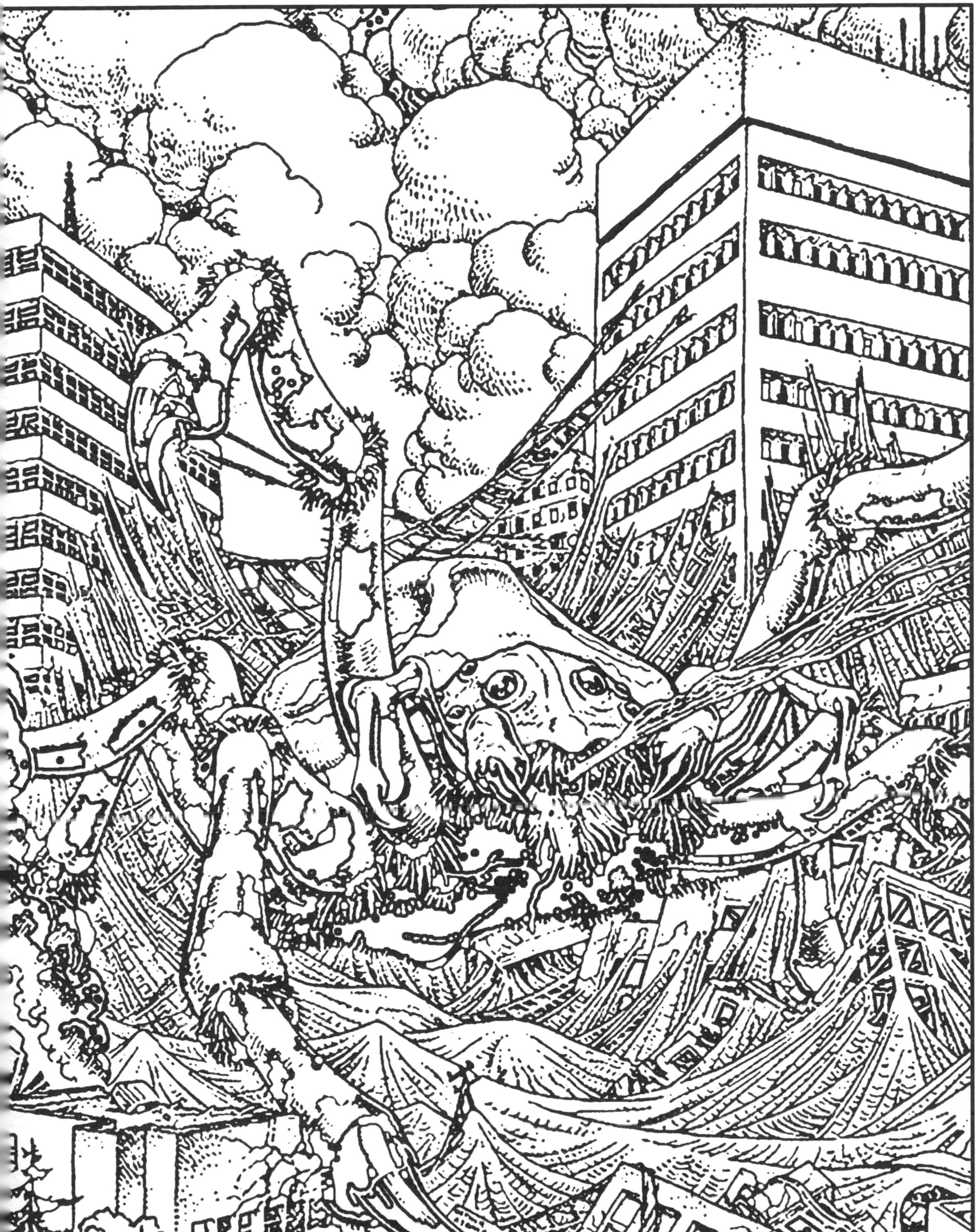

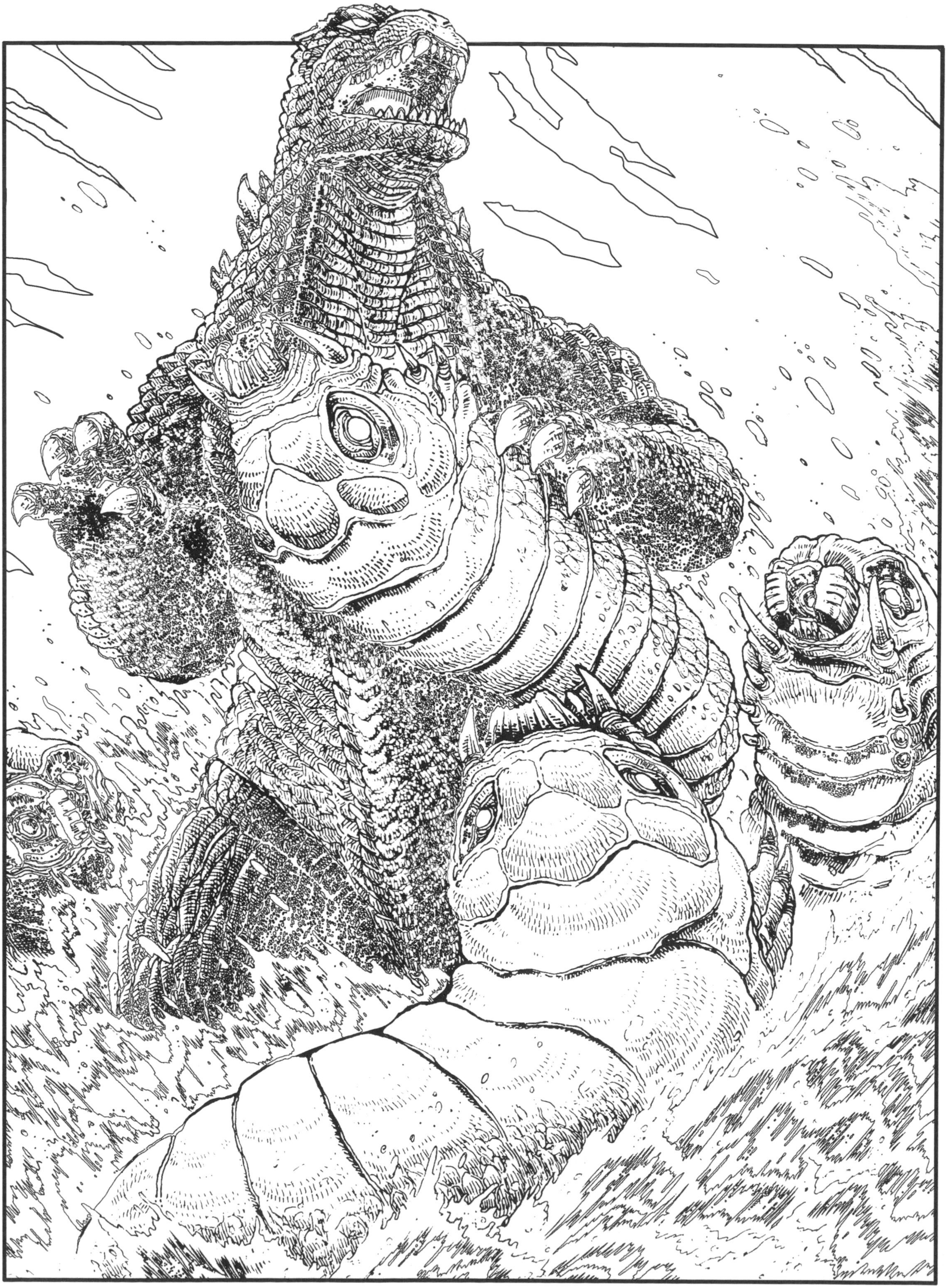

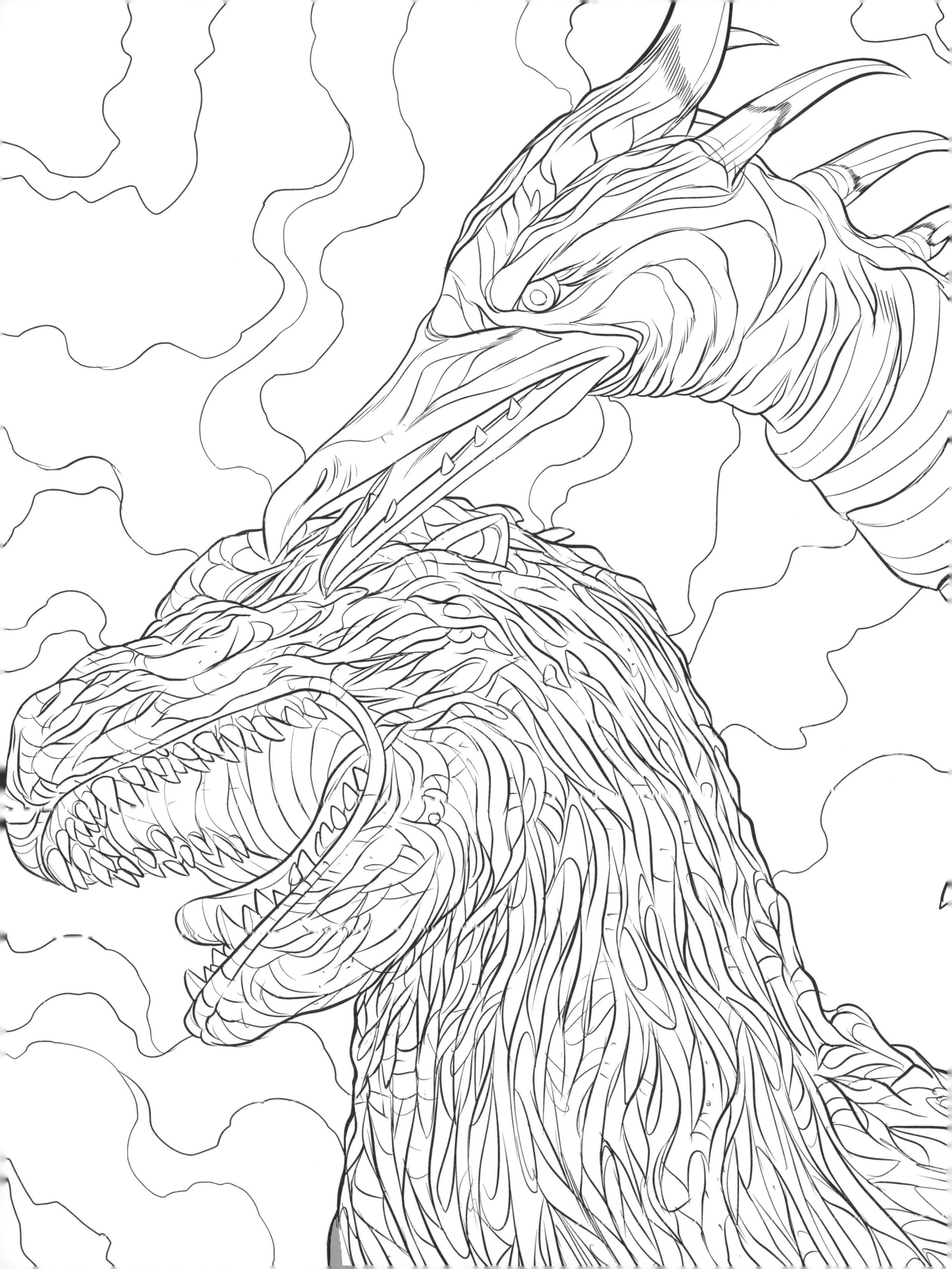

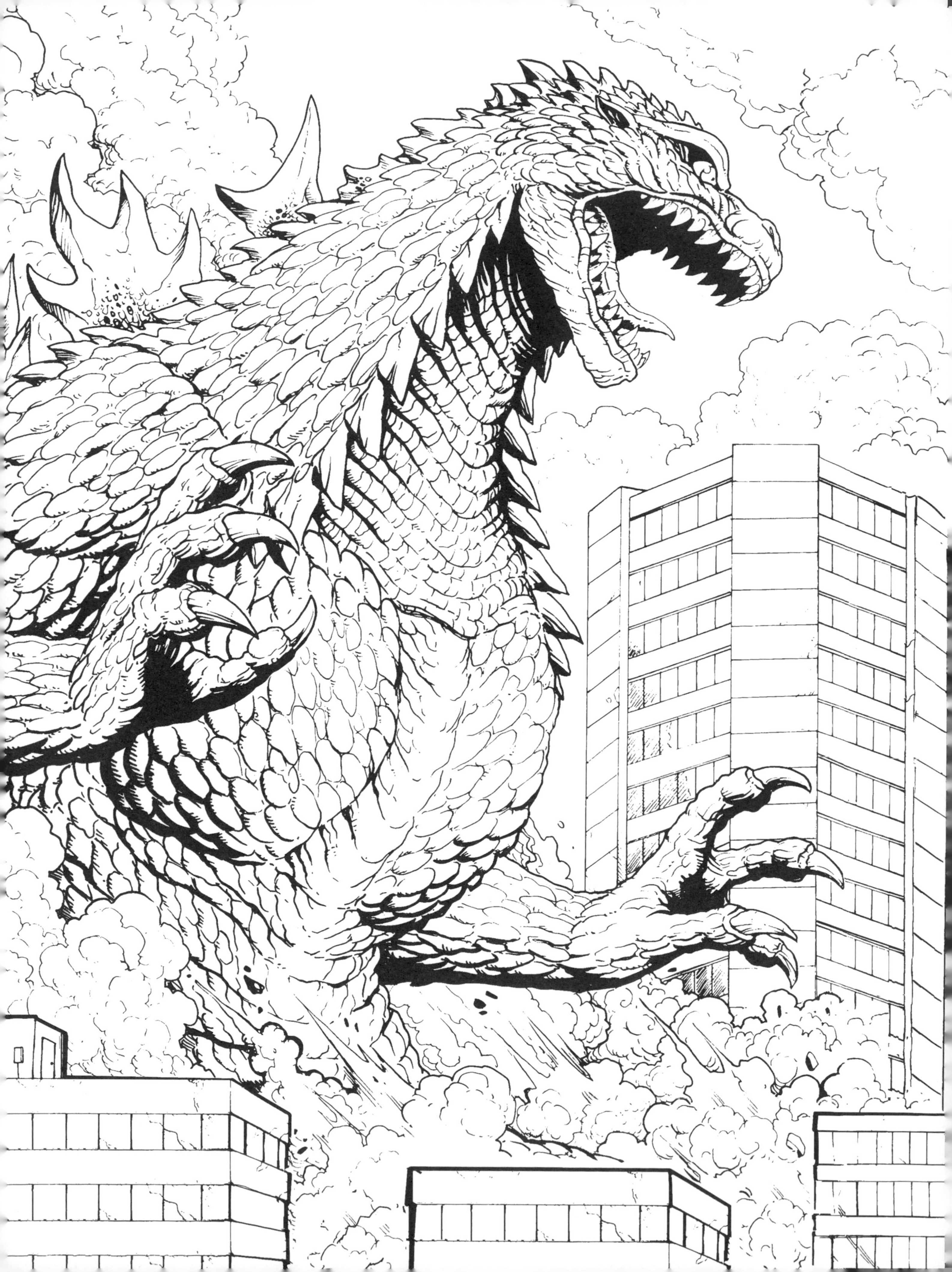

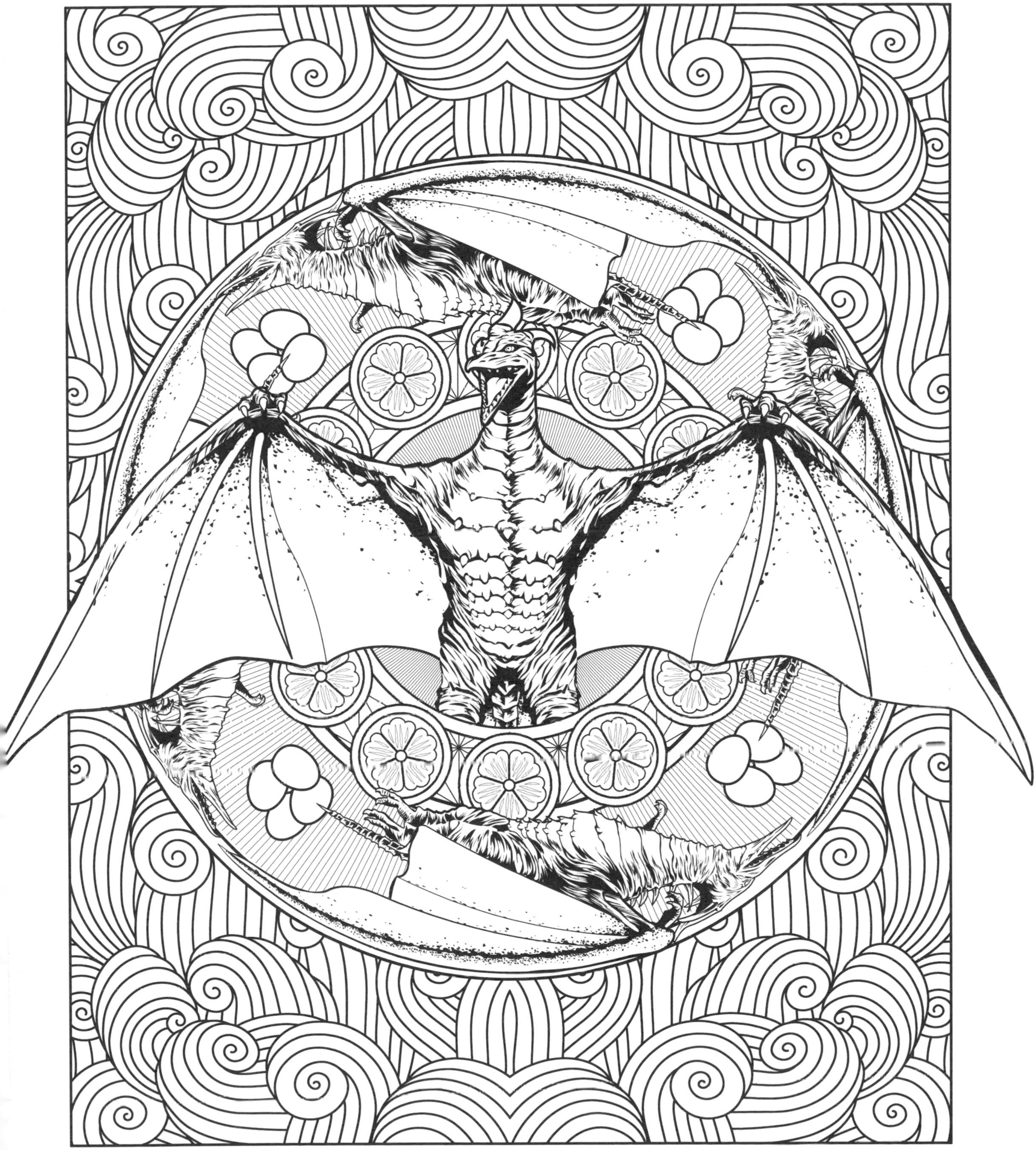

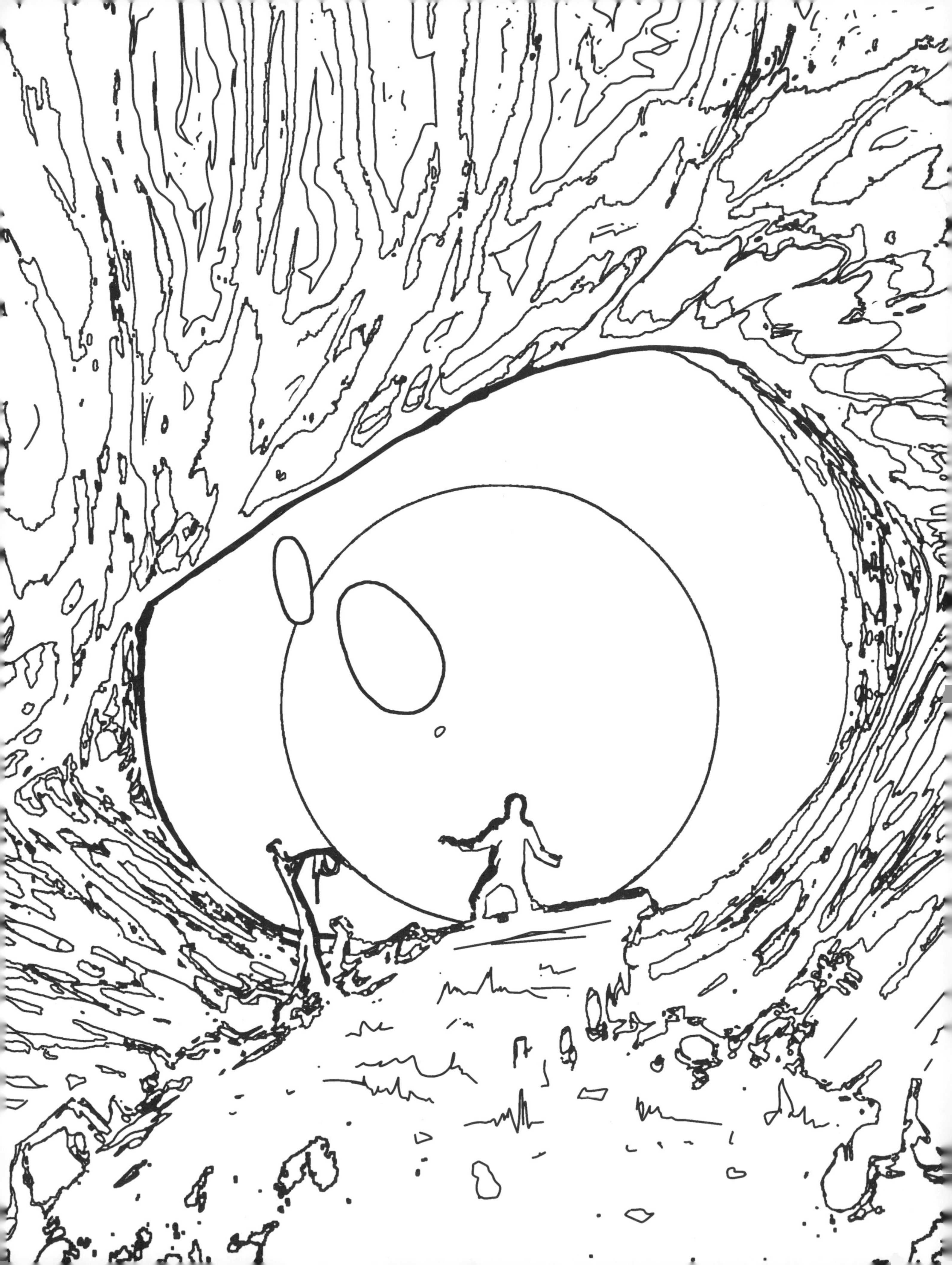

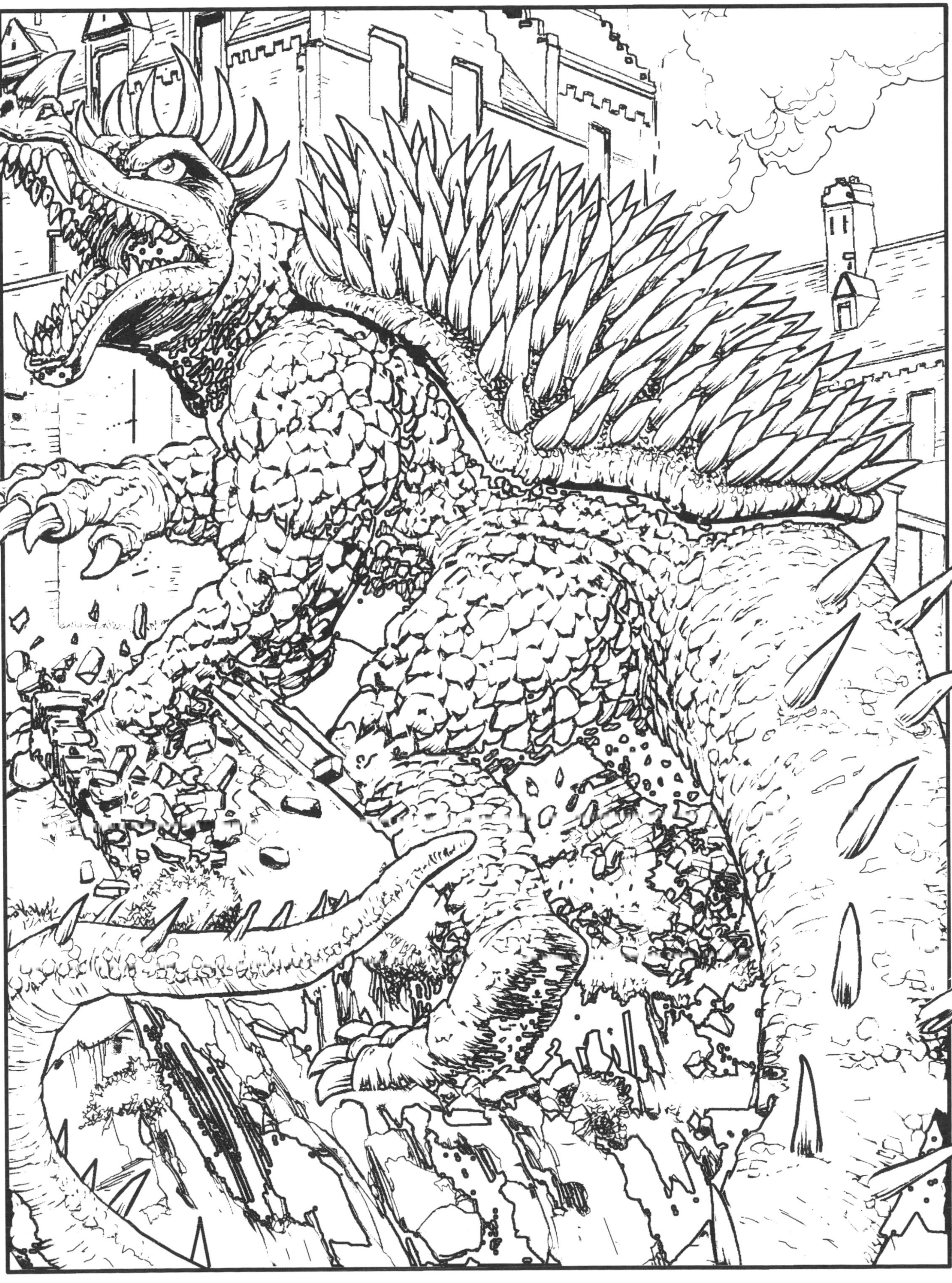

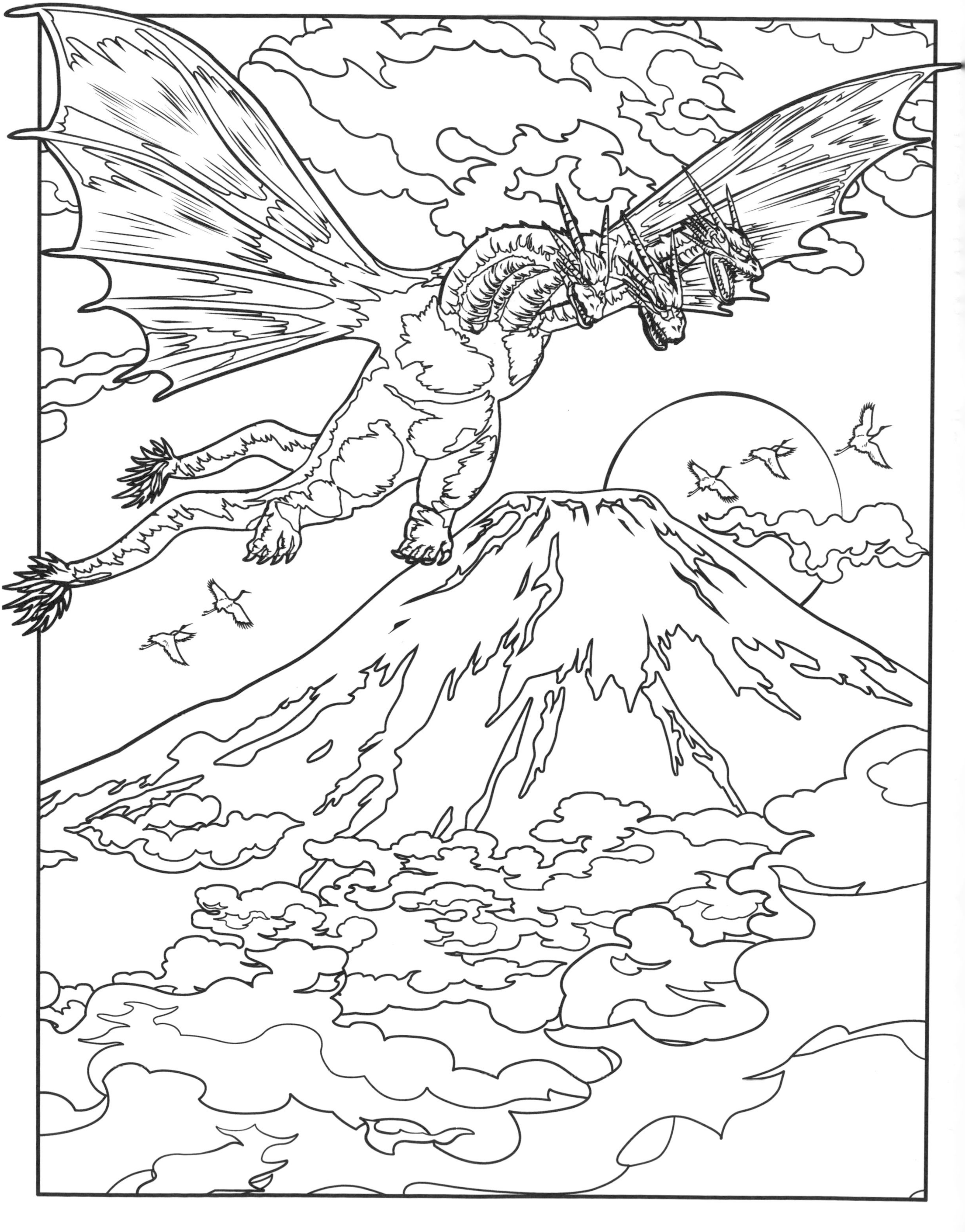

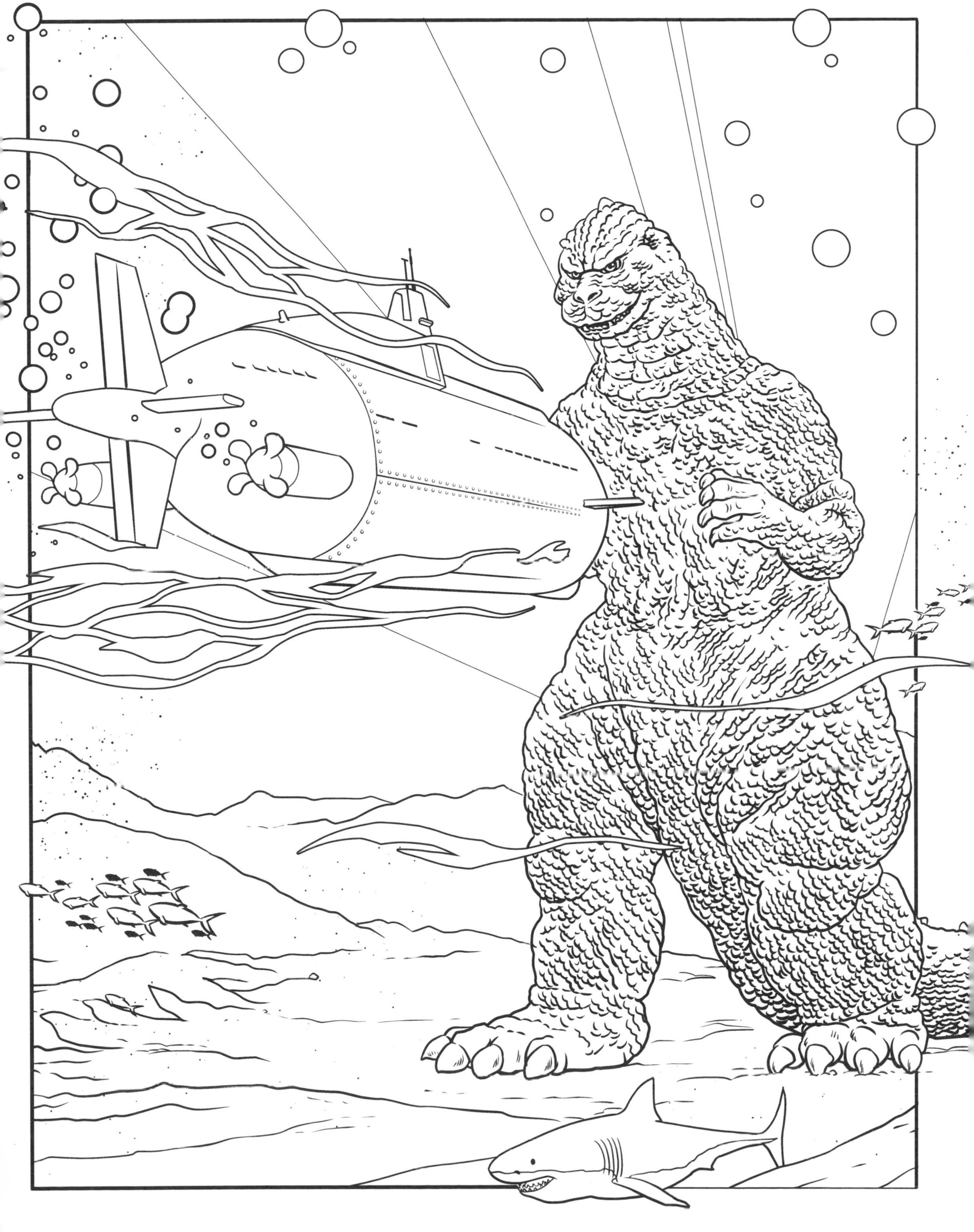

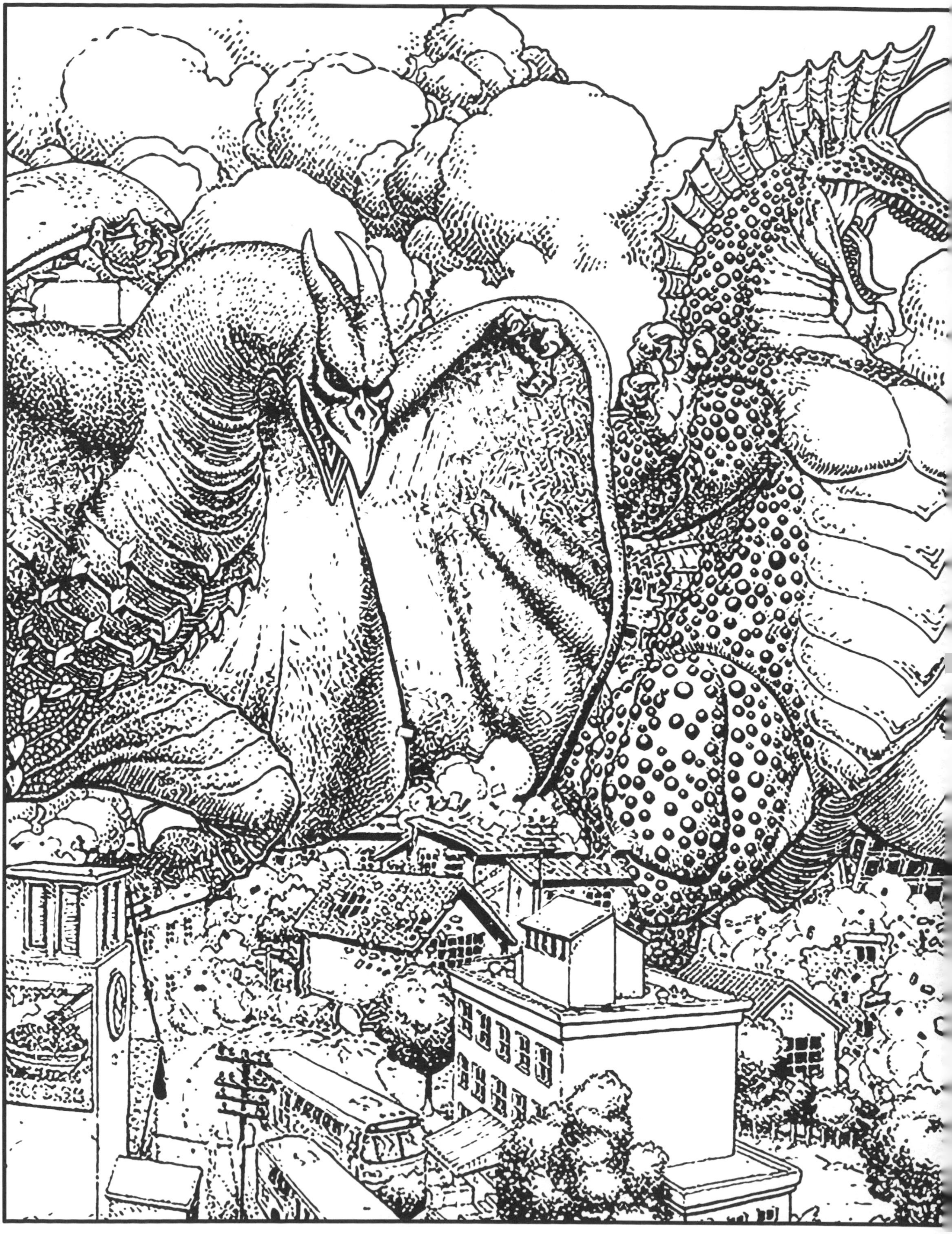

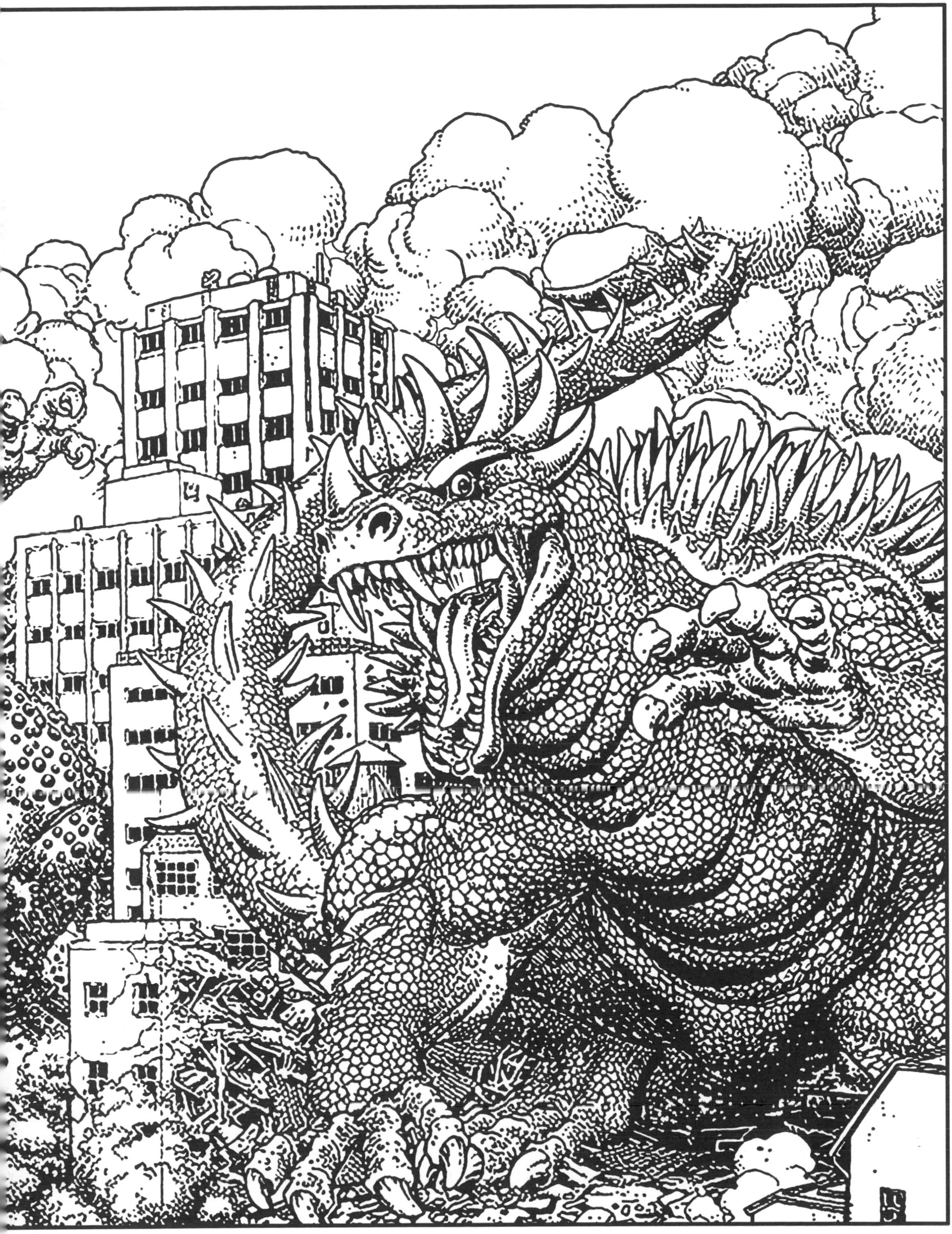

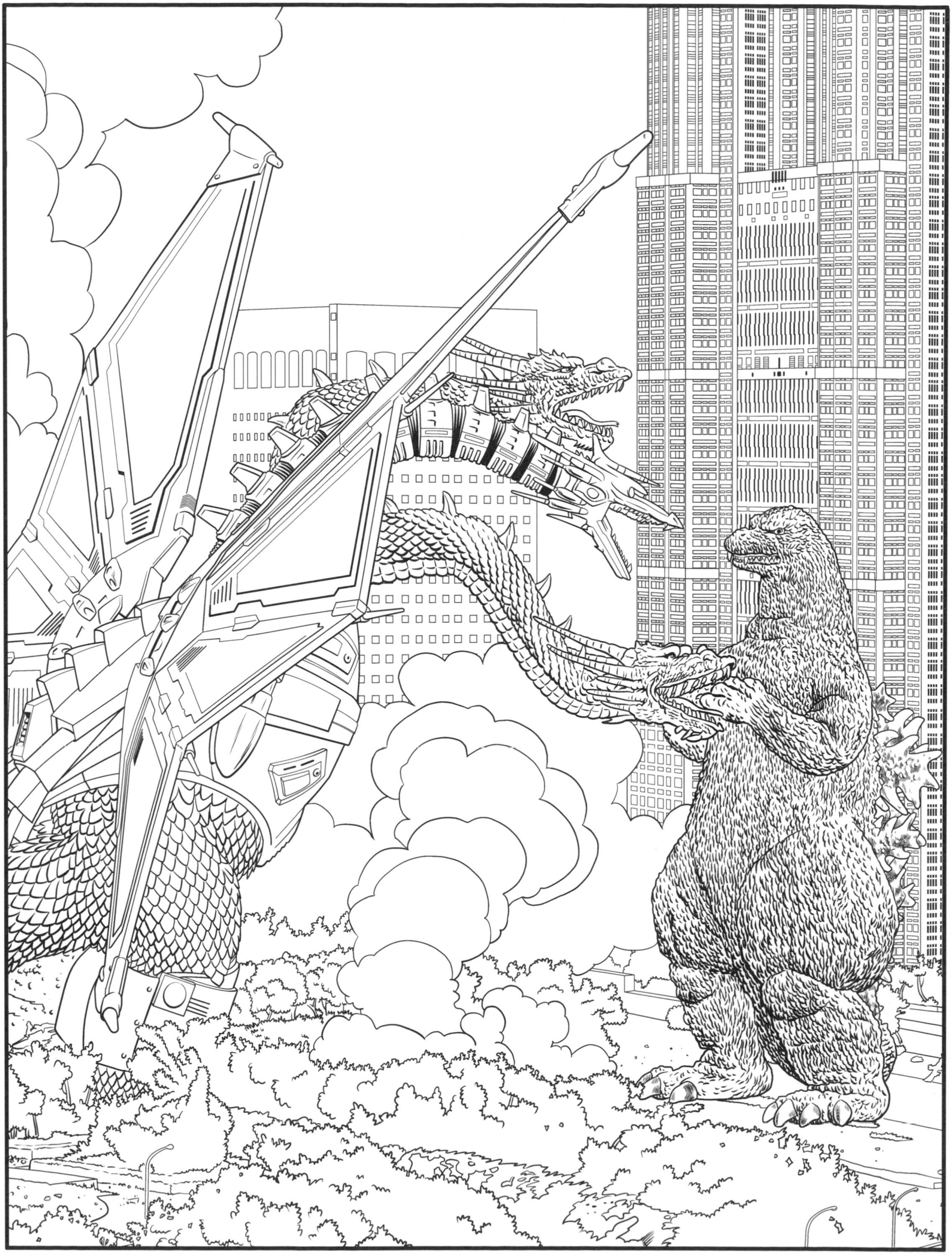

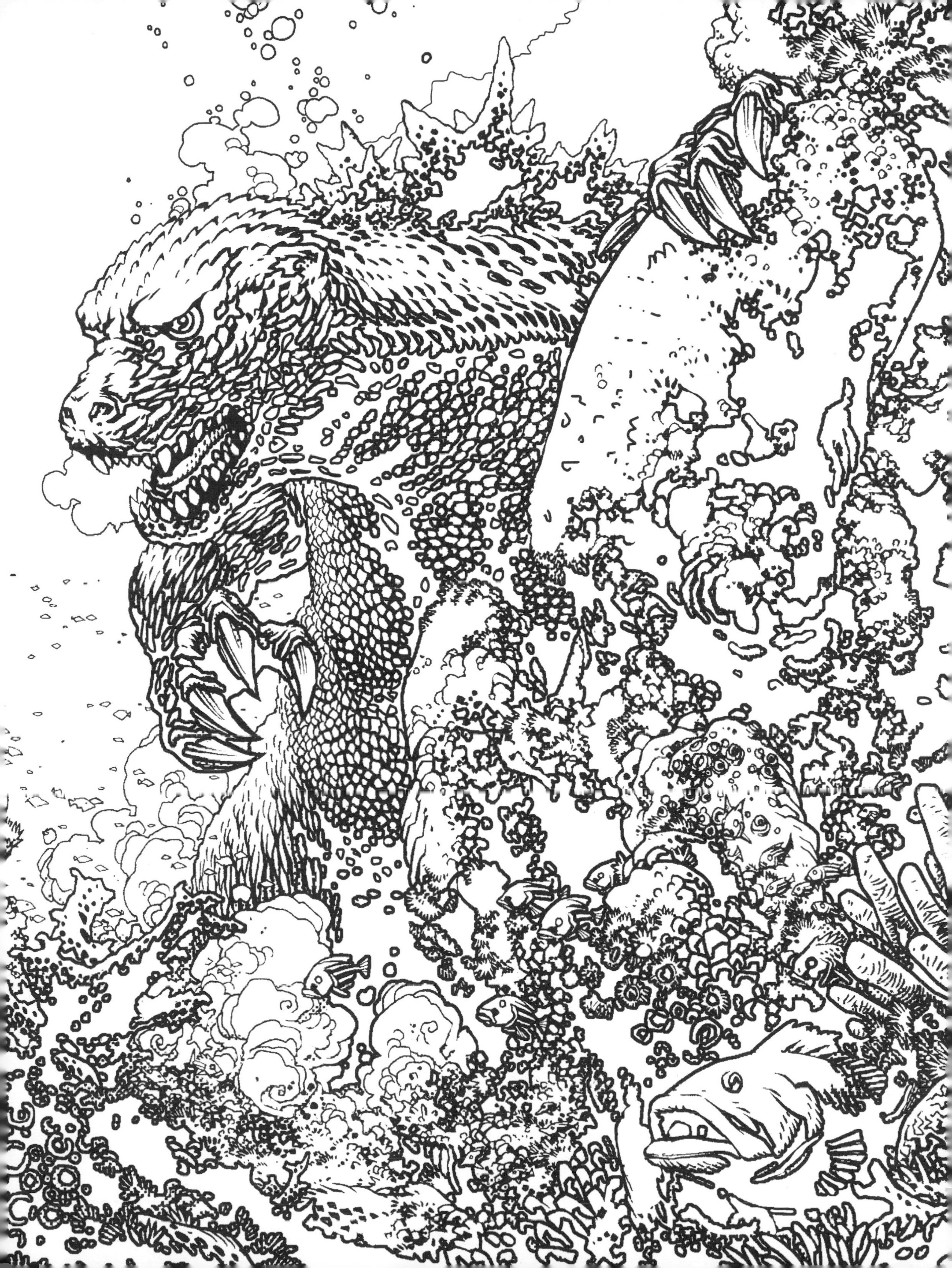

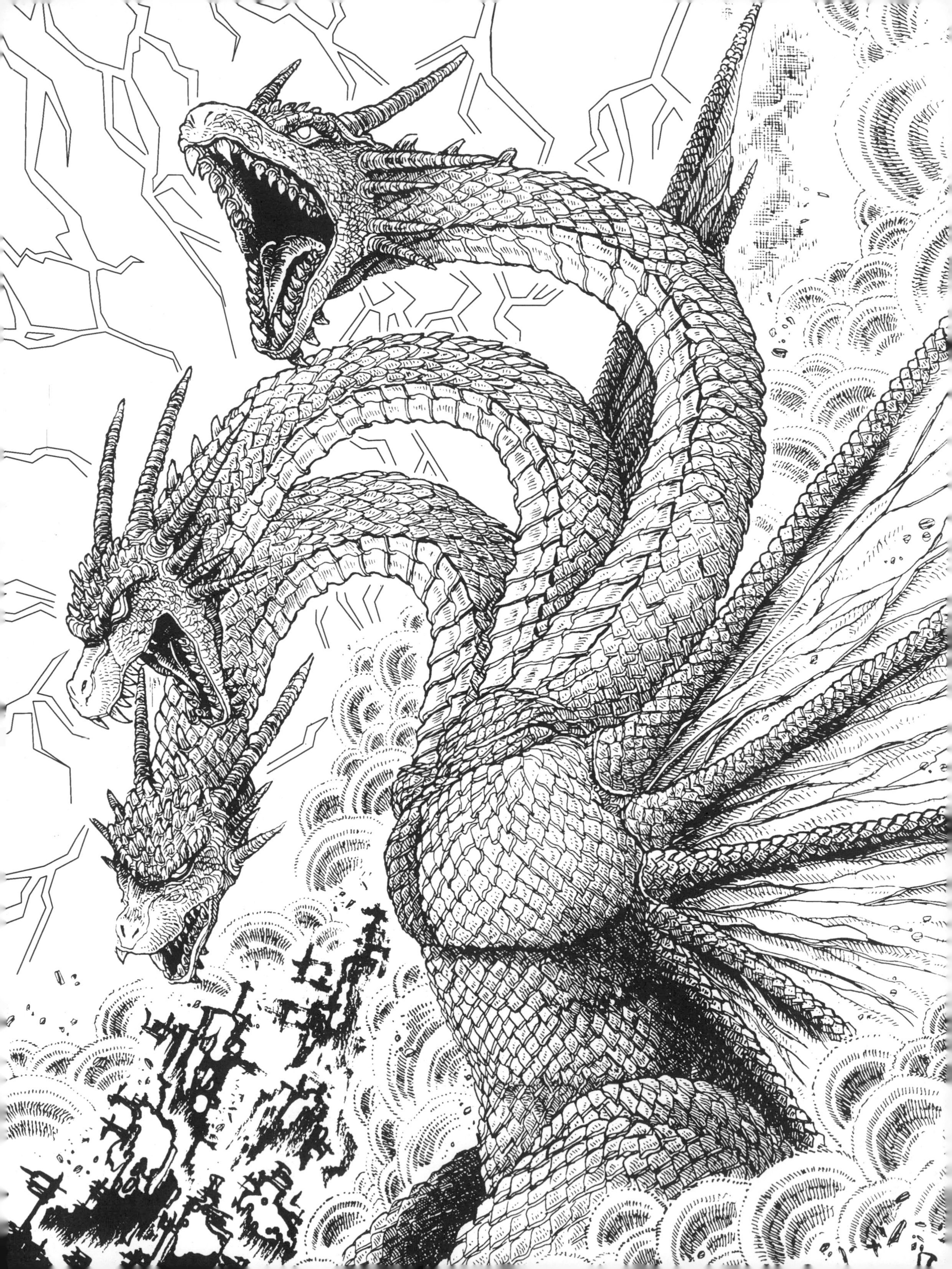

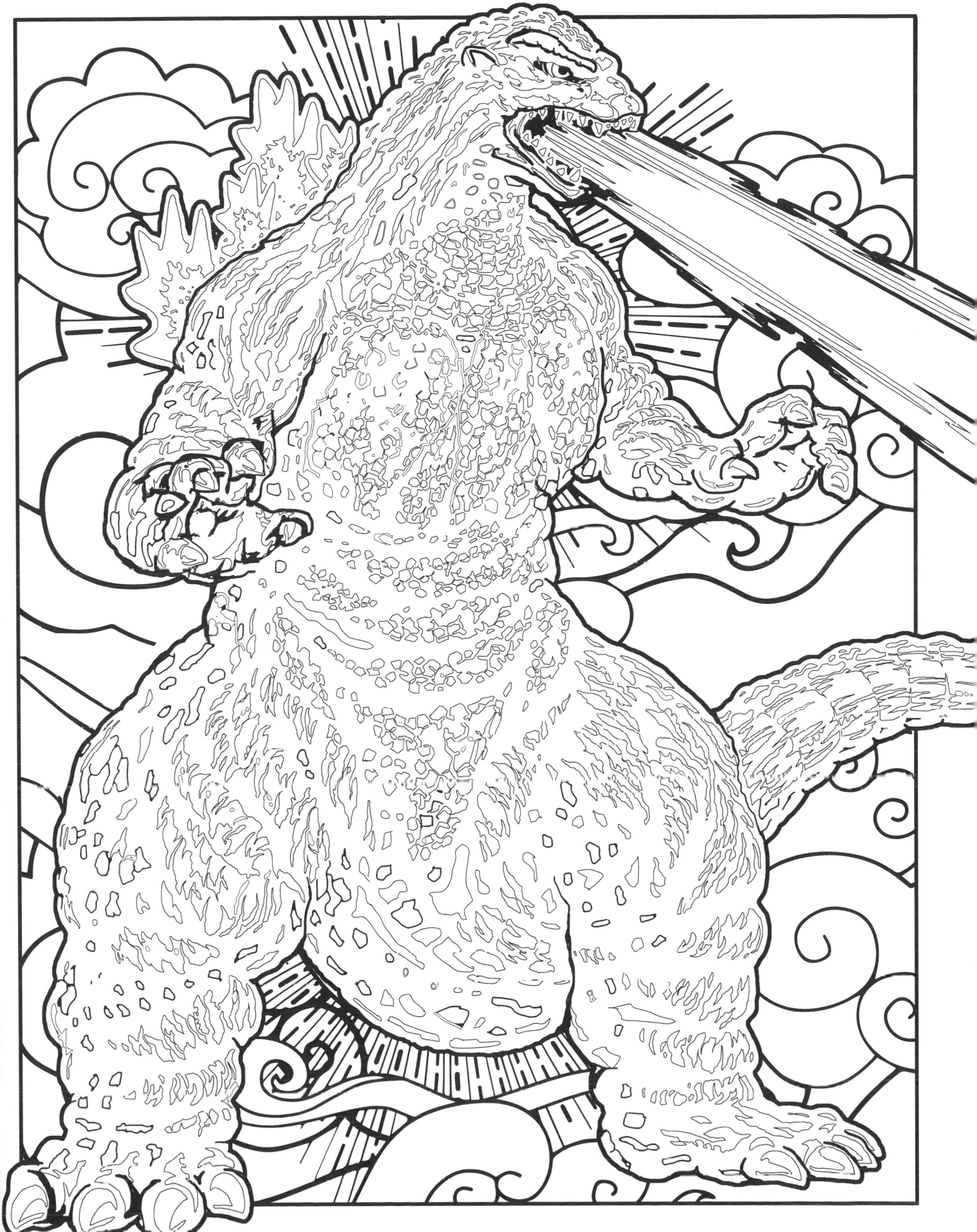

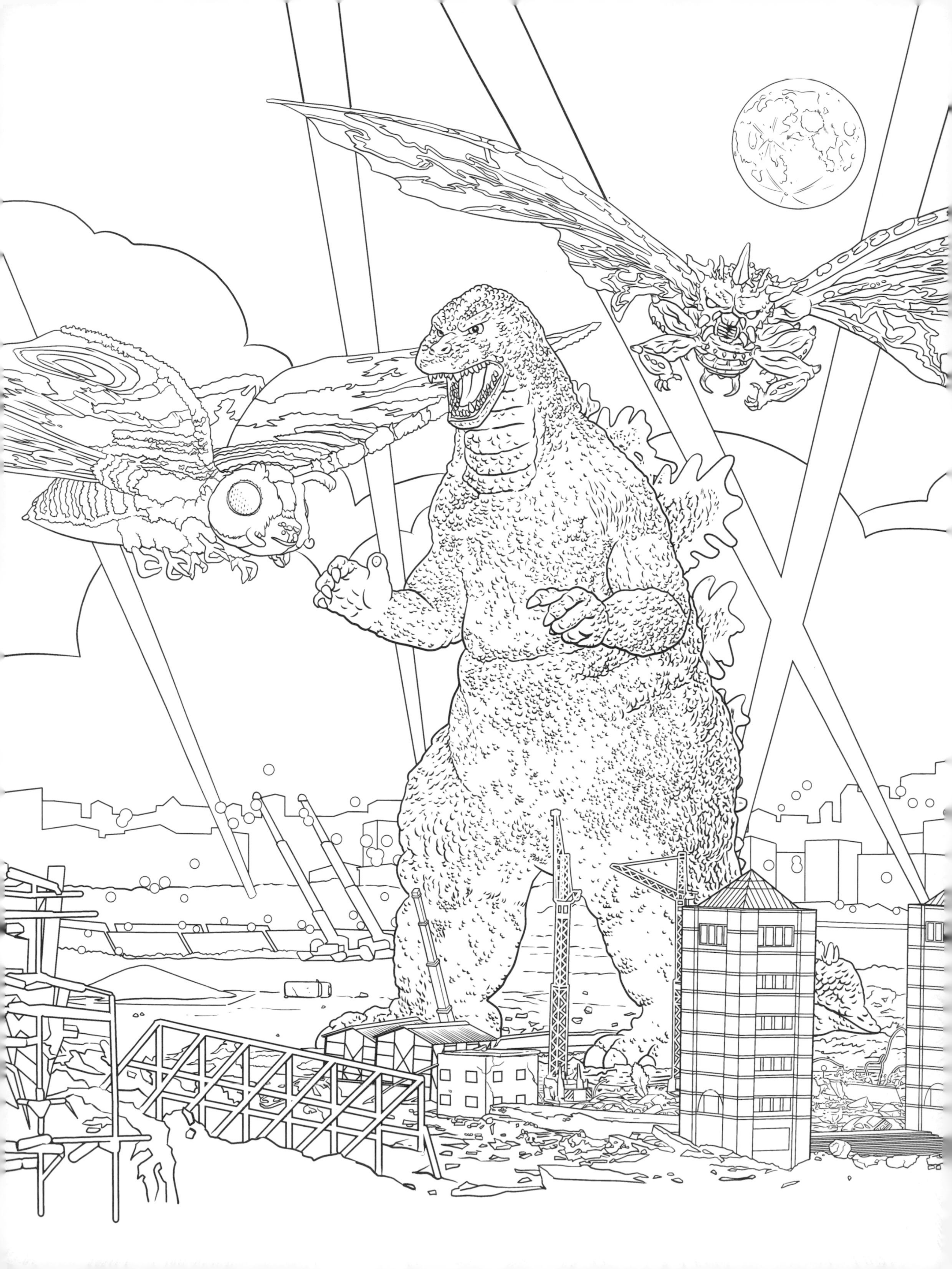

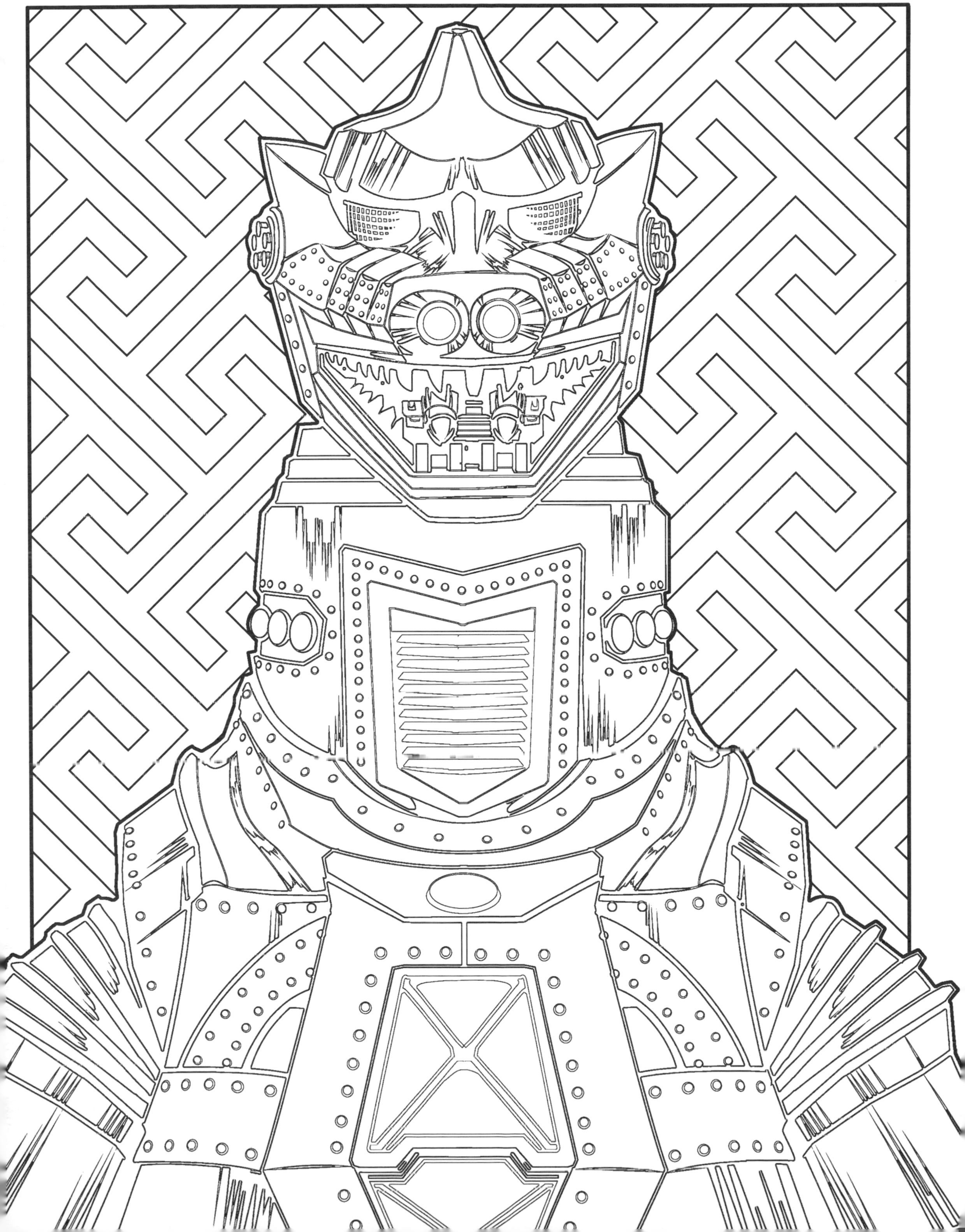

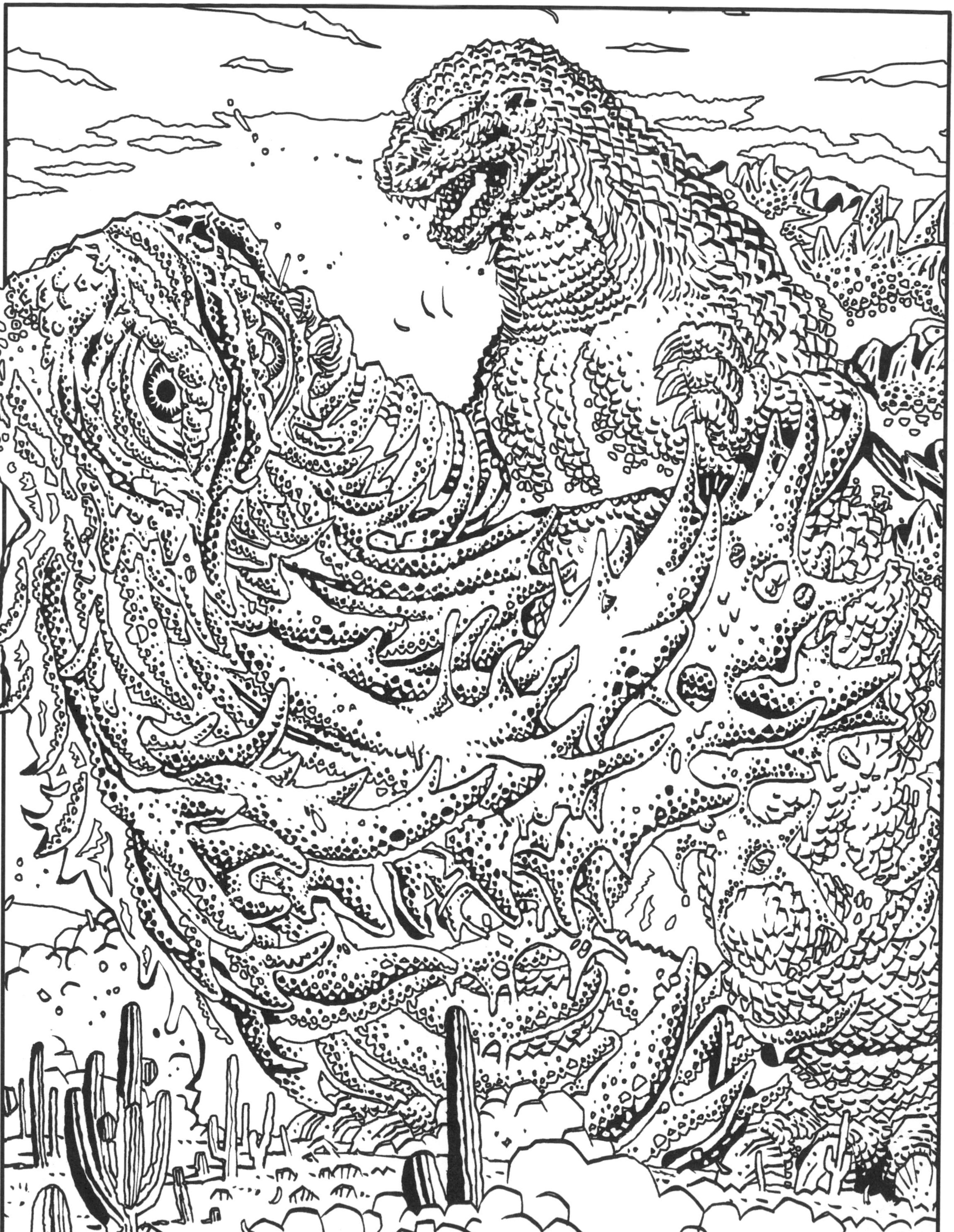

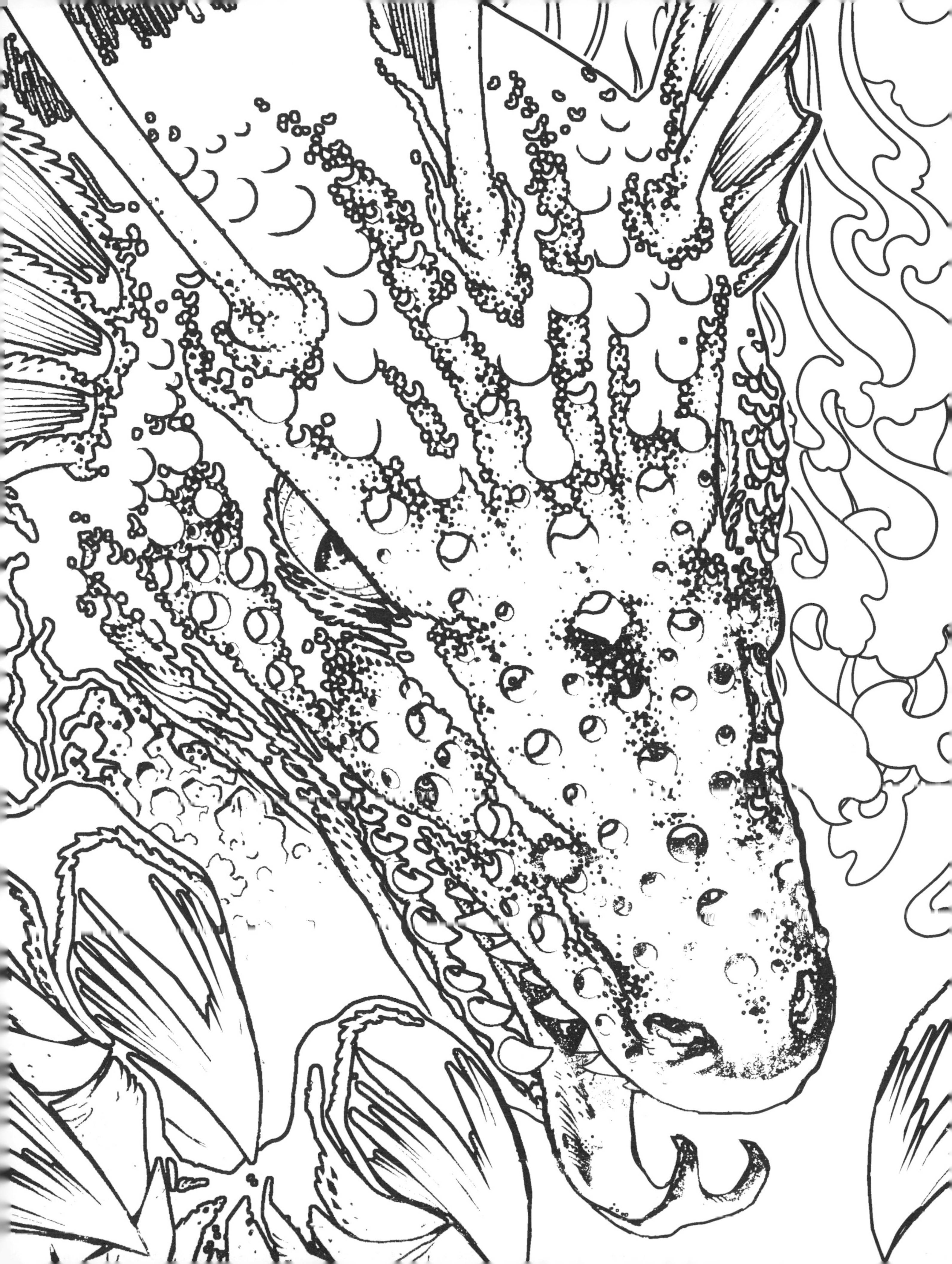

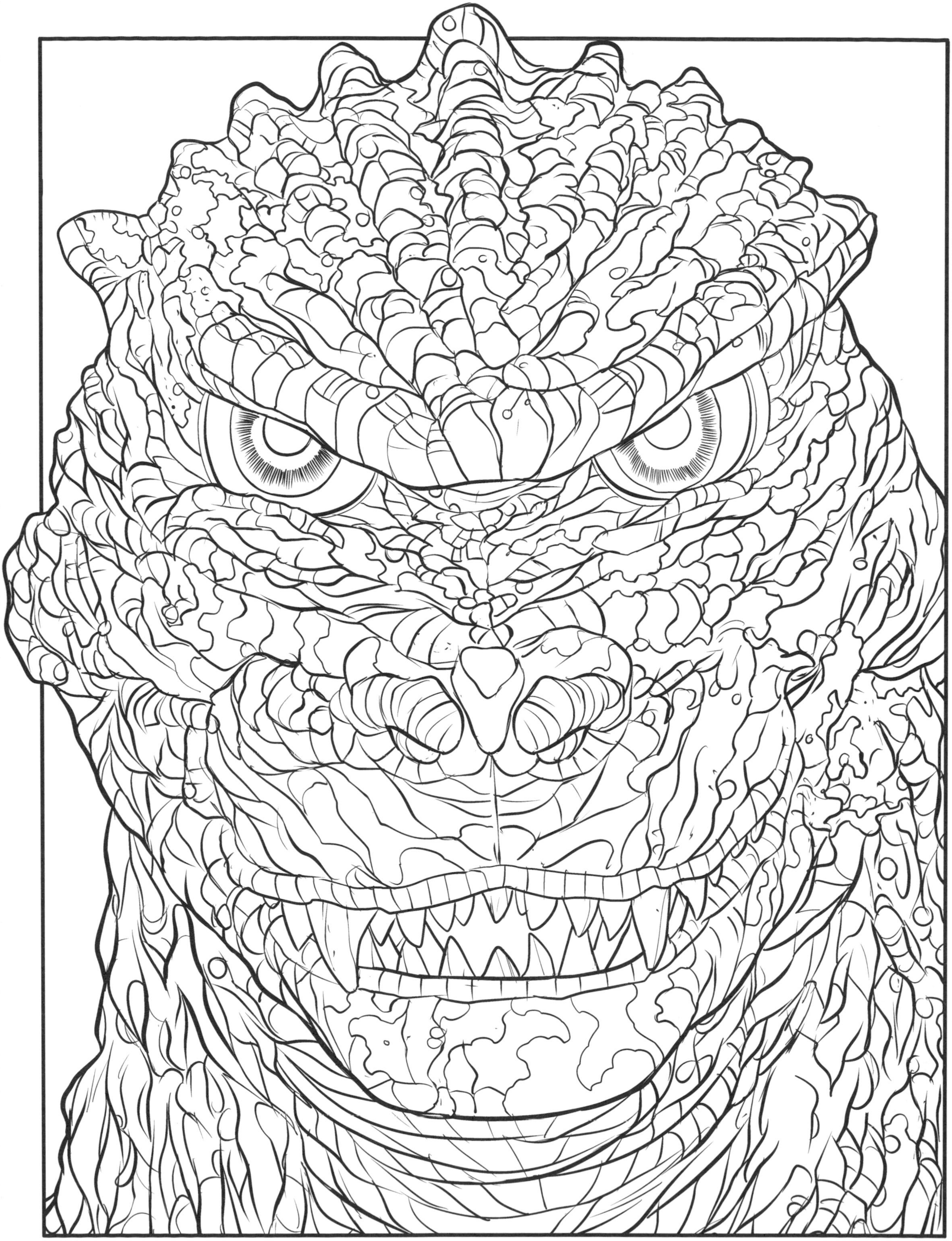

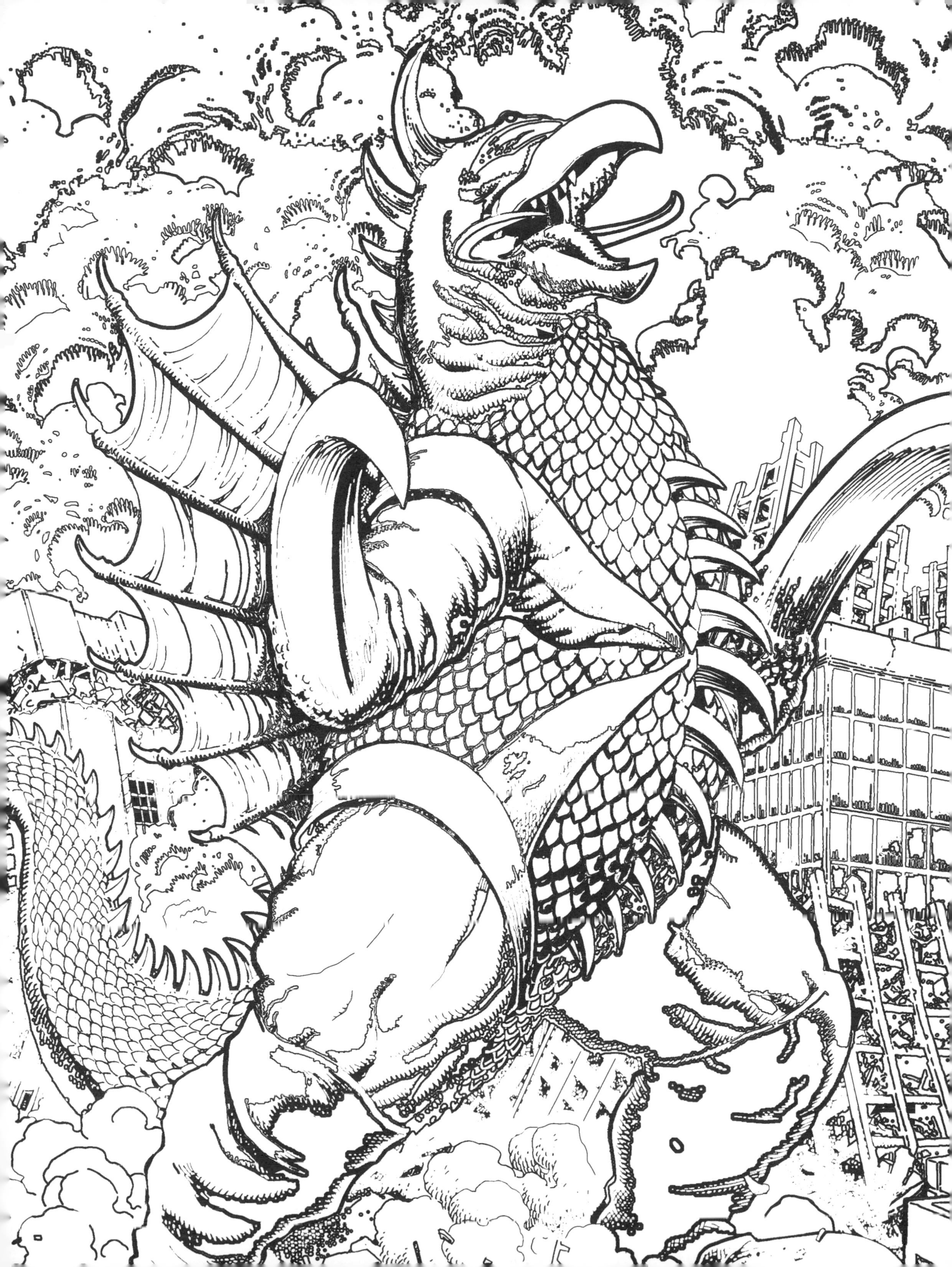

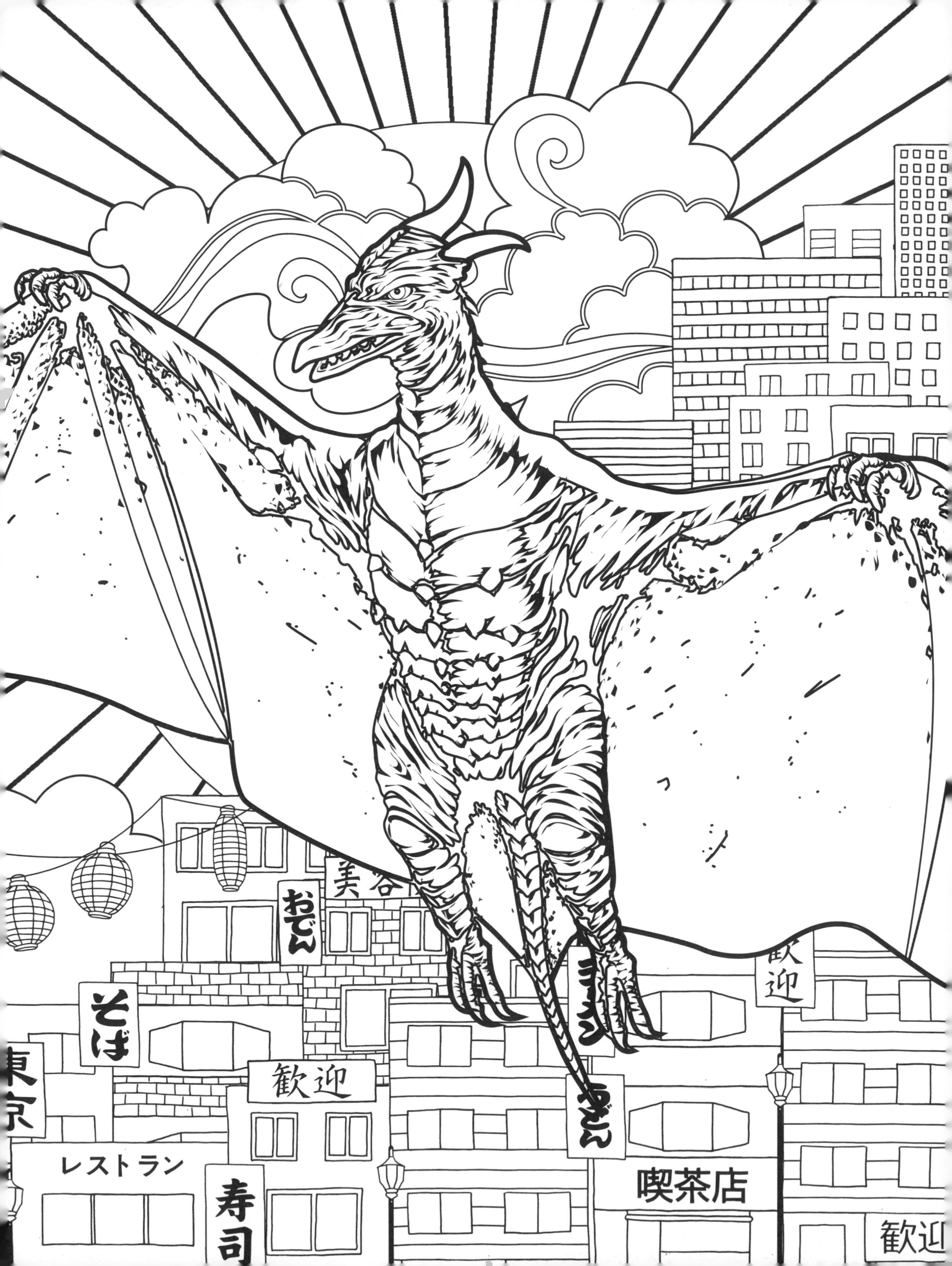
おでん
そば
歓迎
レストラン
寿司
喫茶店
歓迎

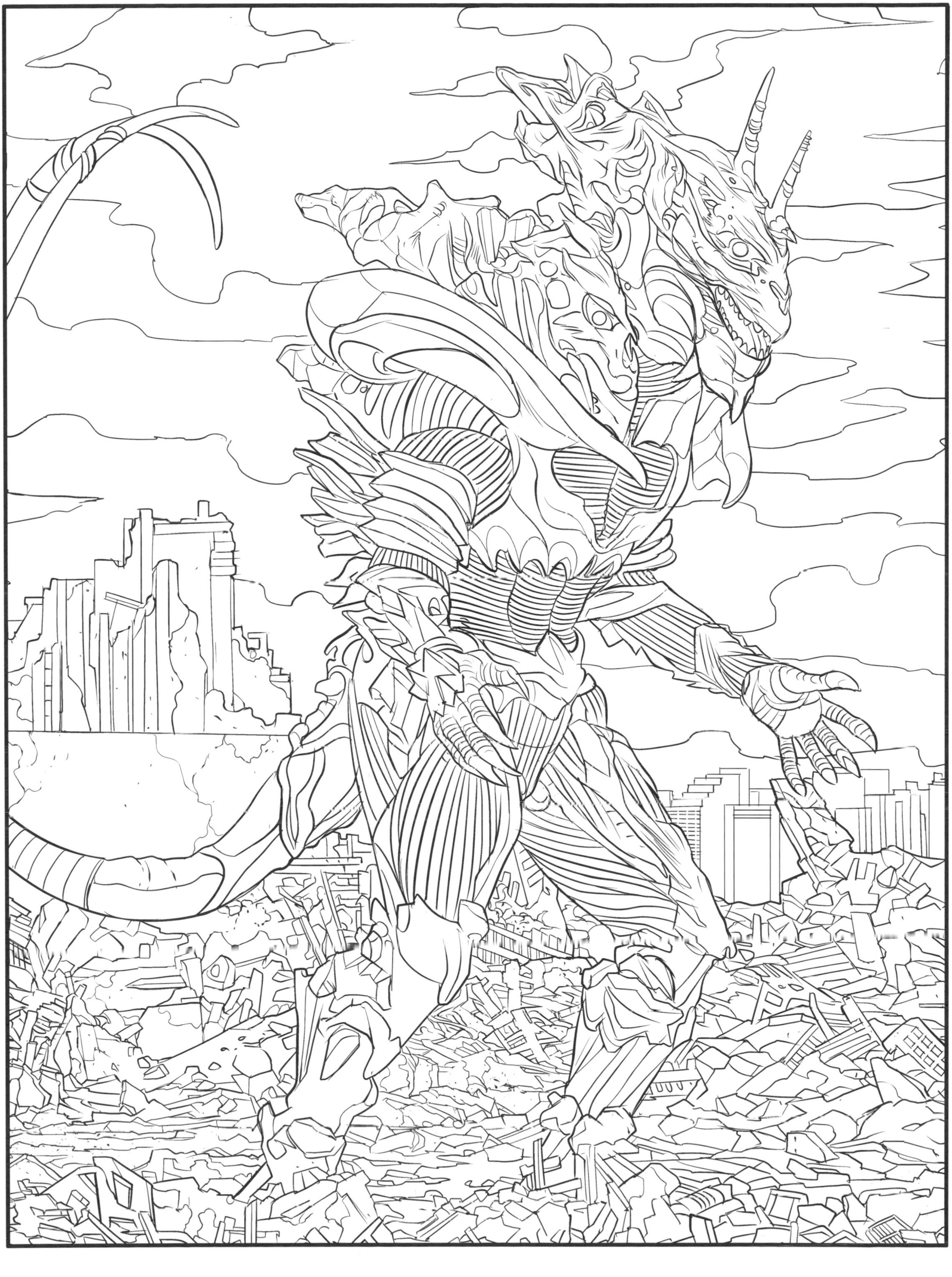

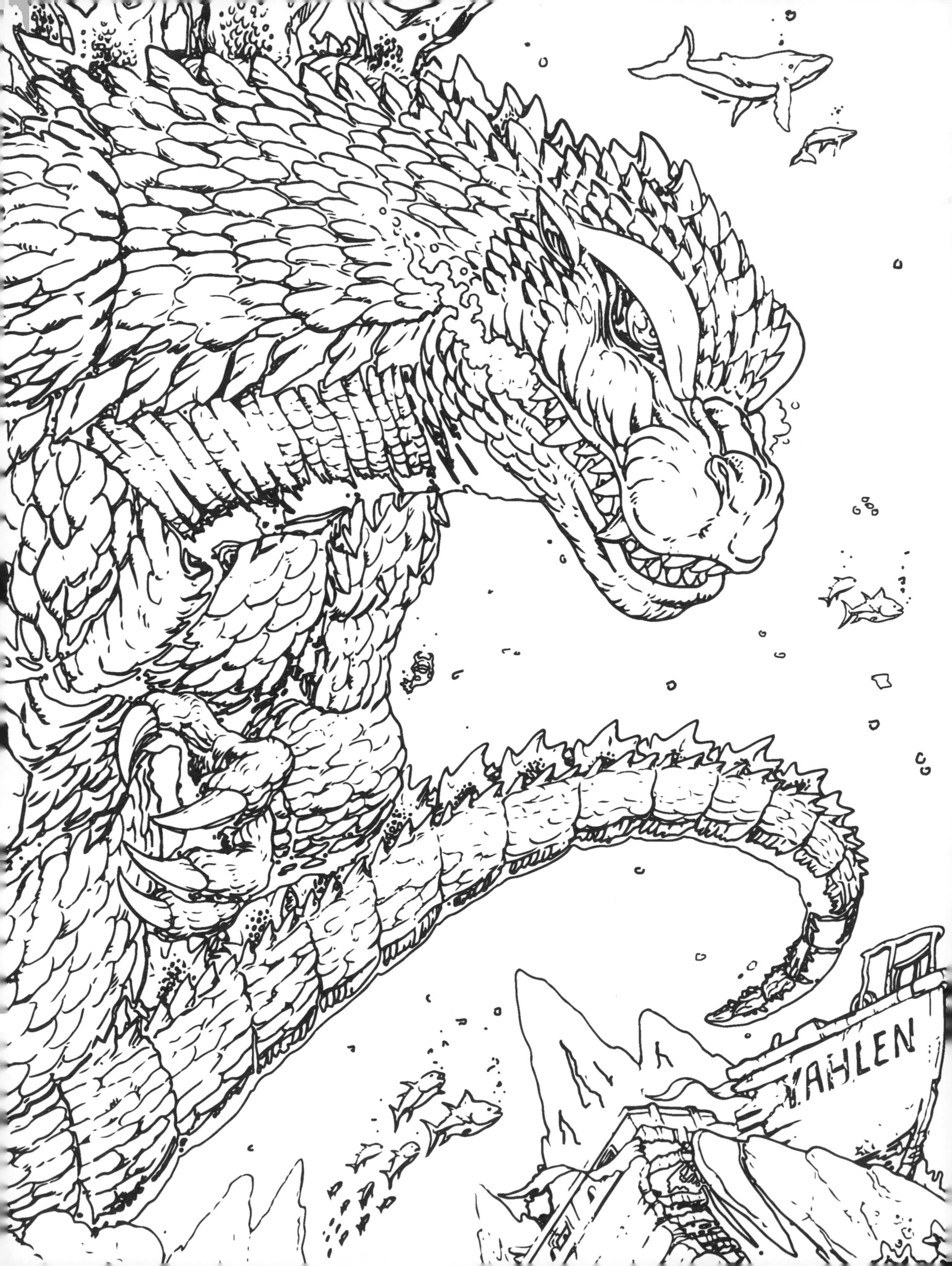
VAHLEN

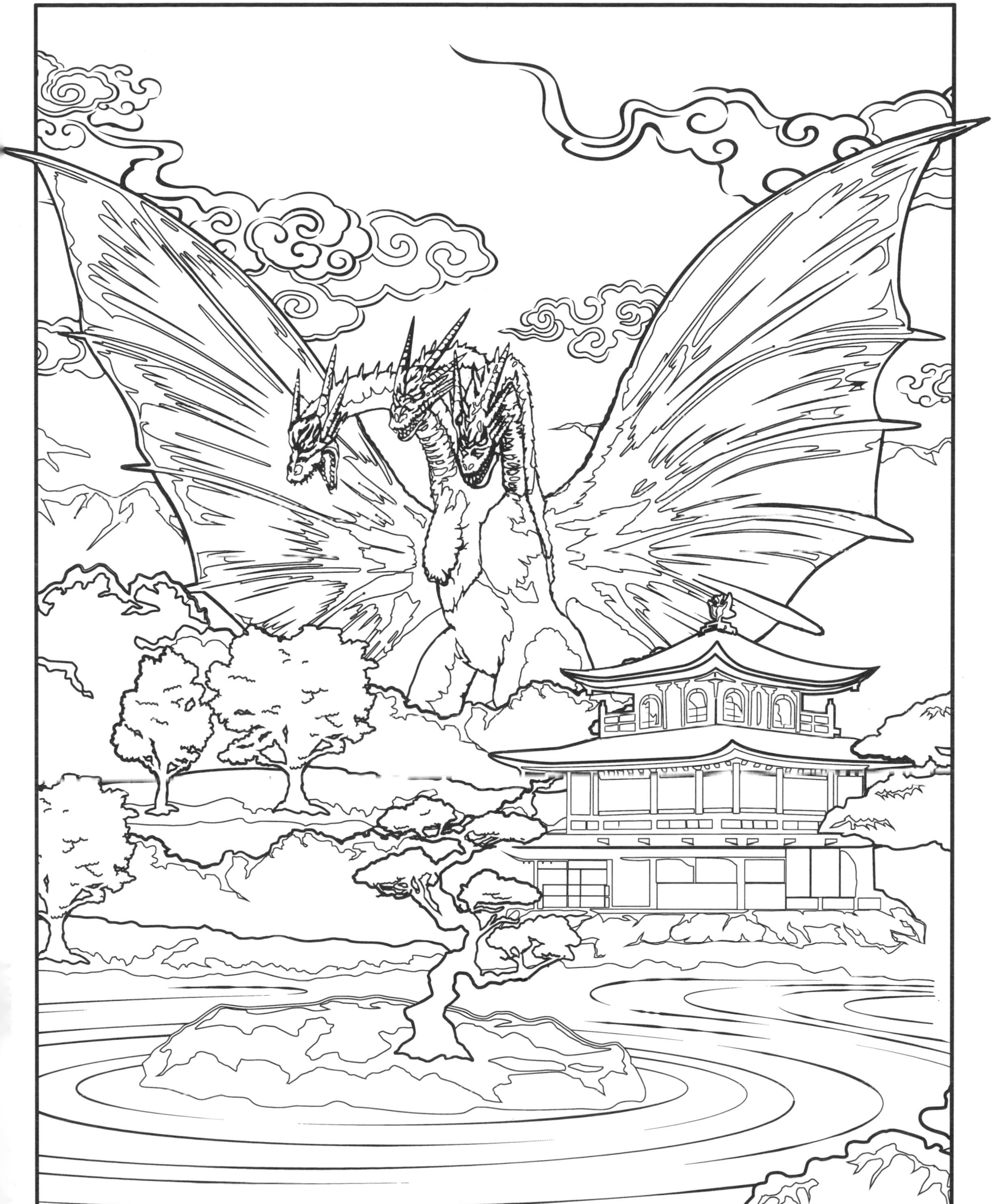

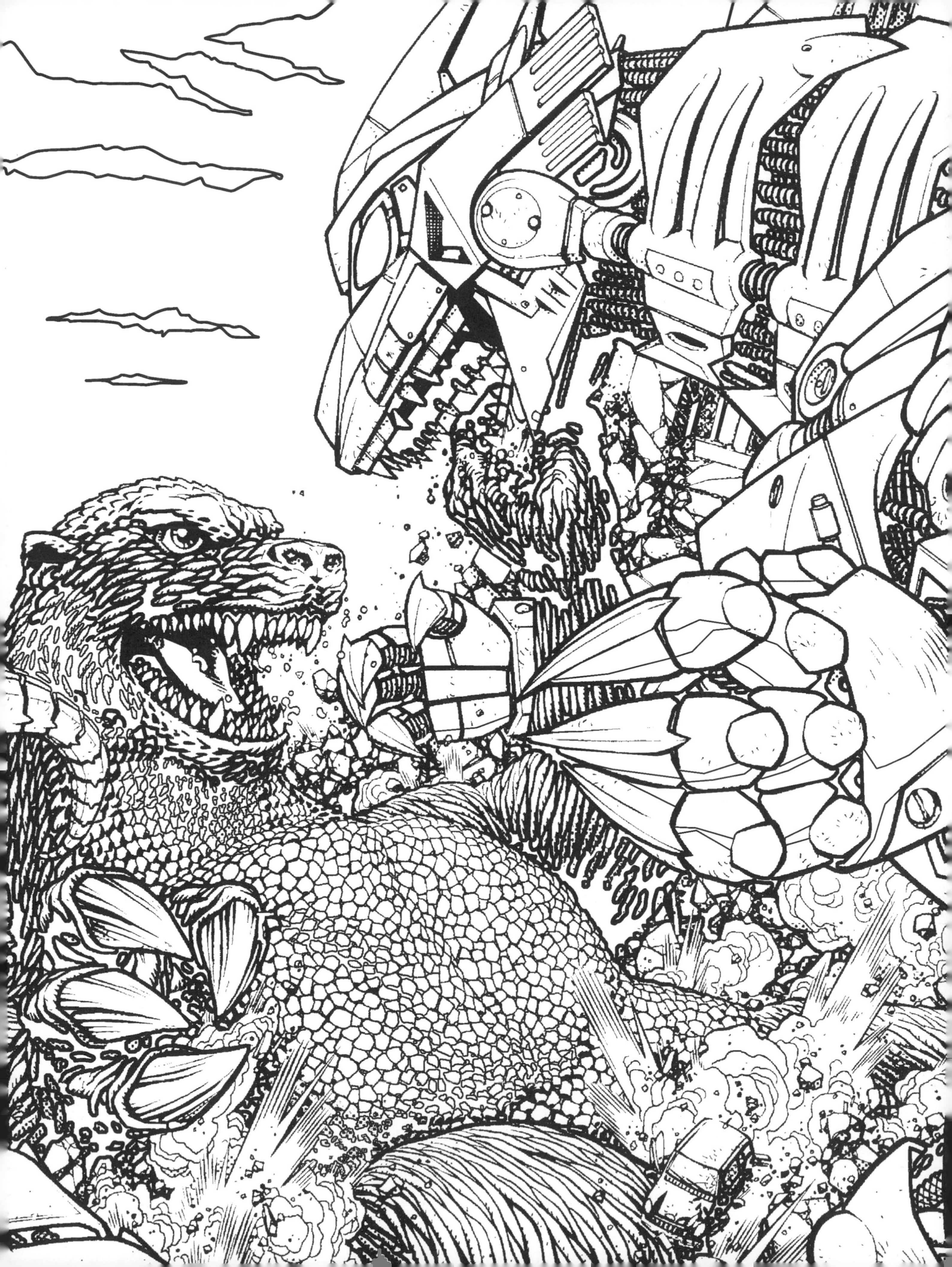

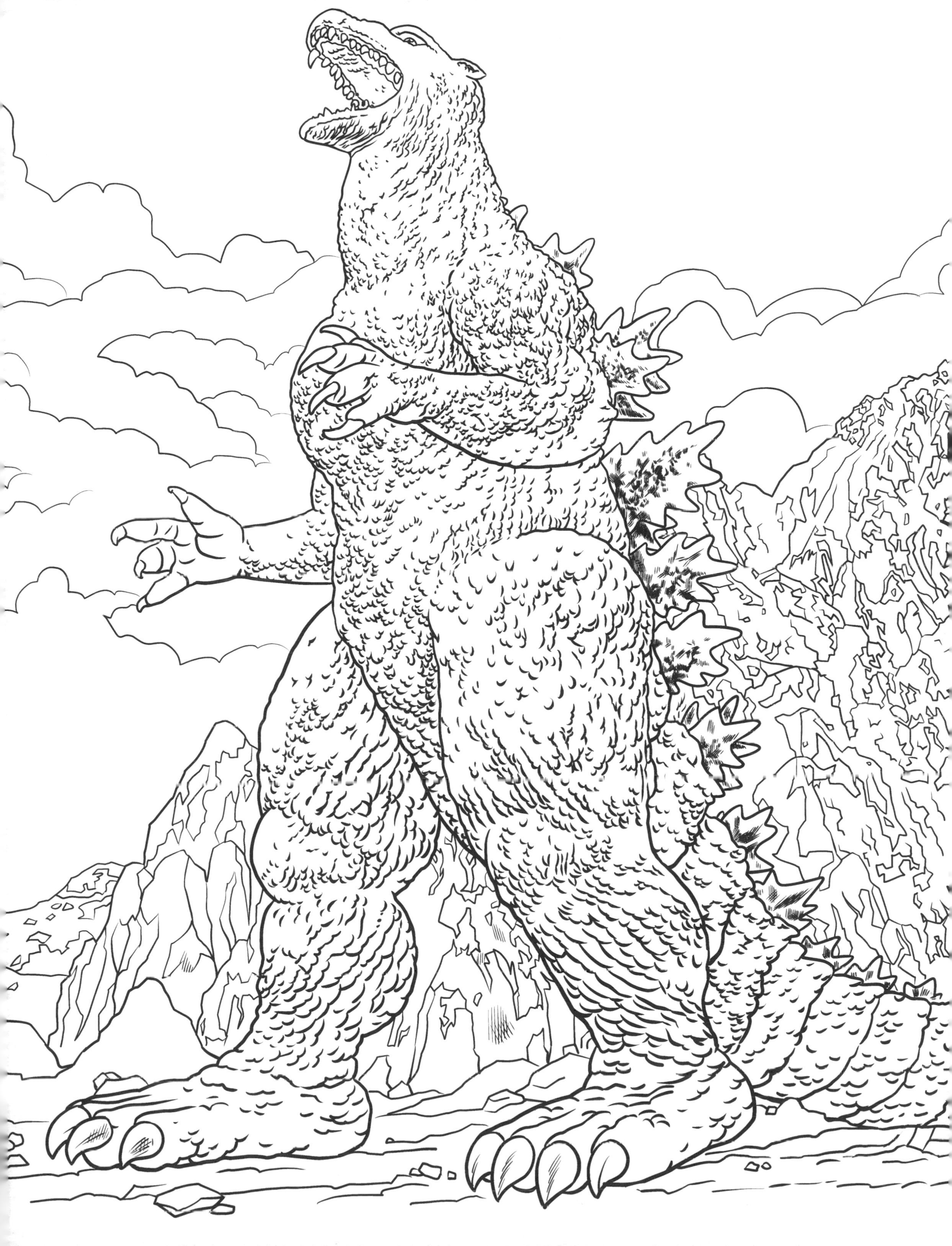

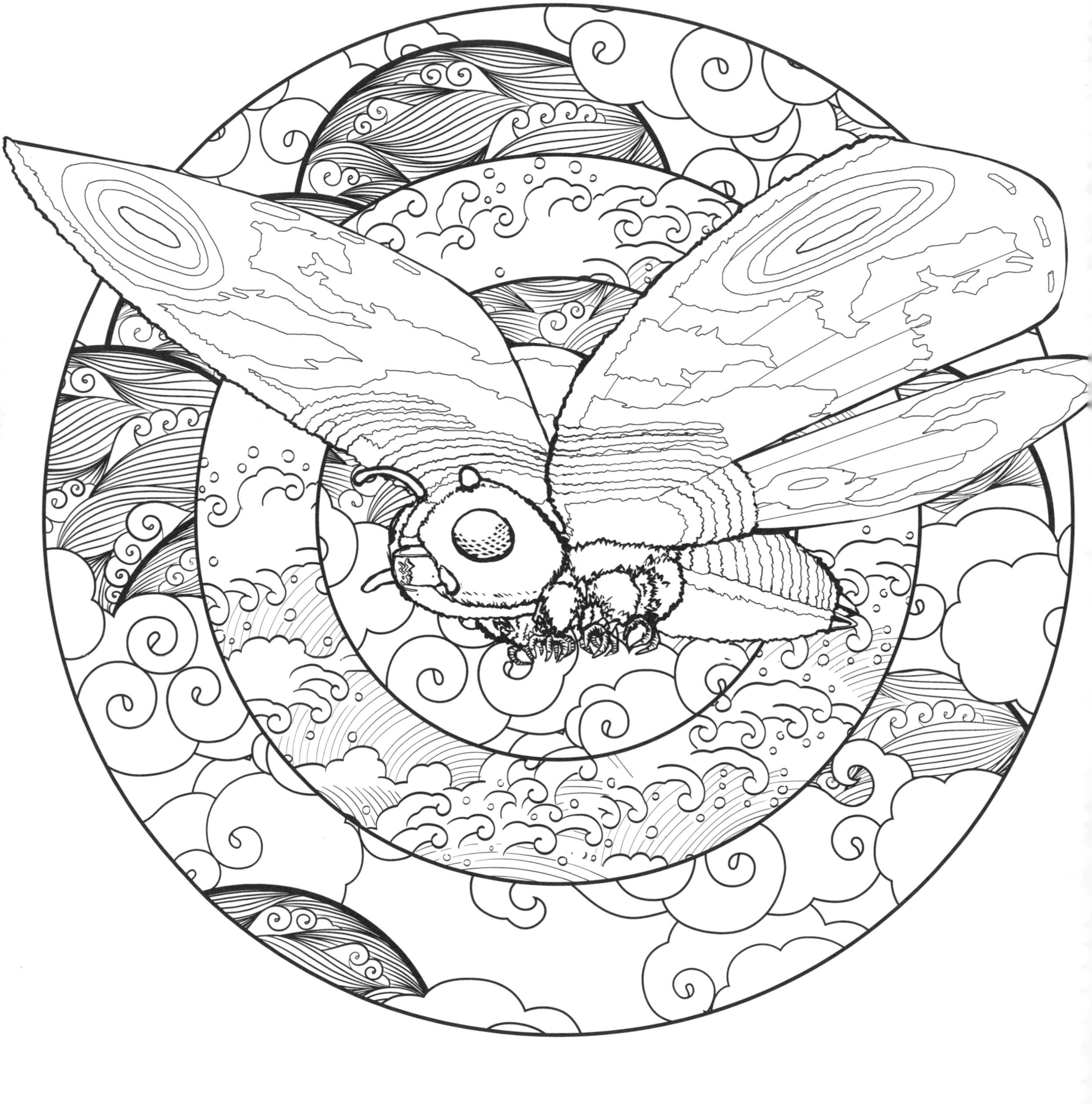

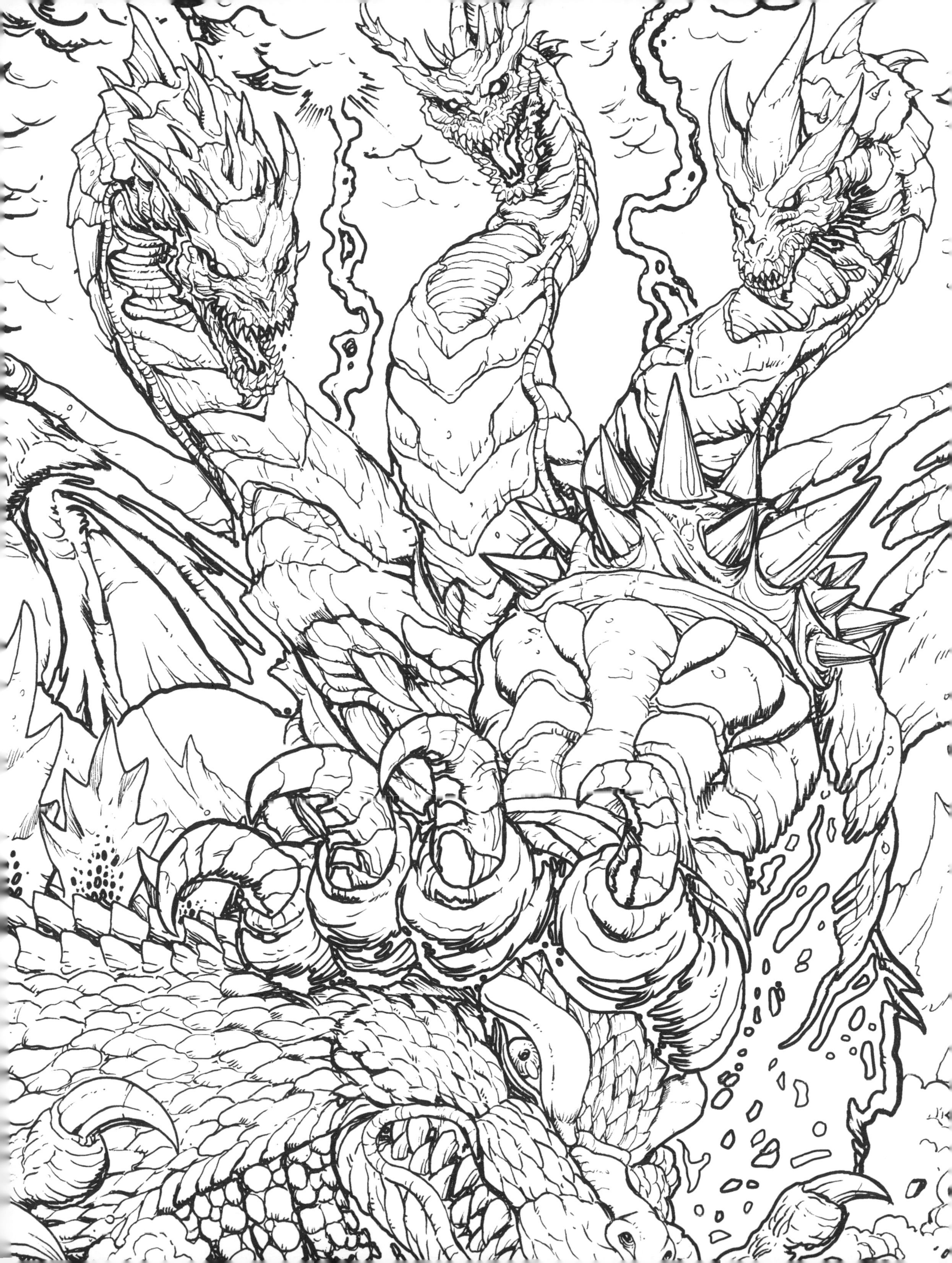

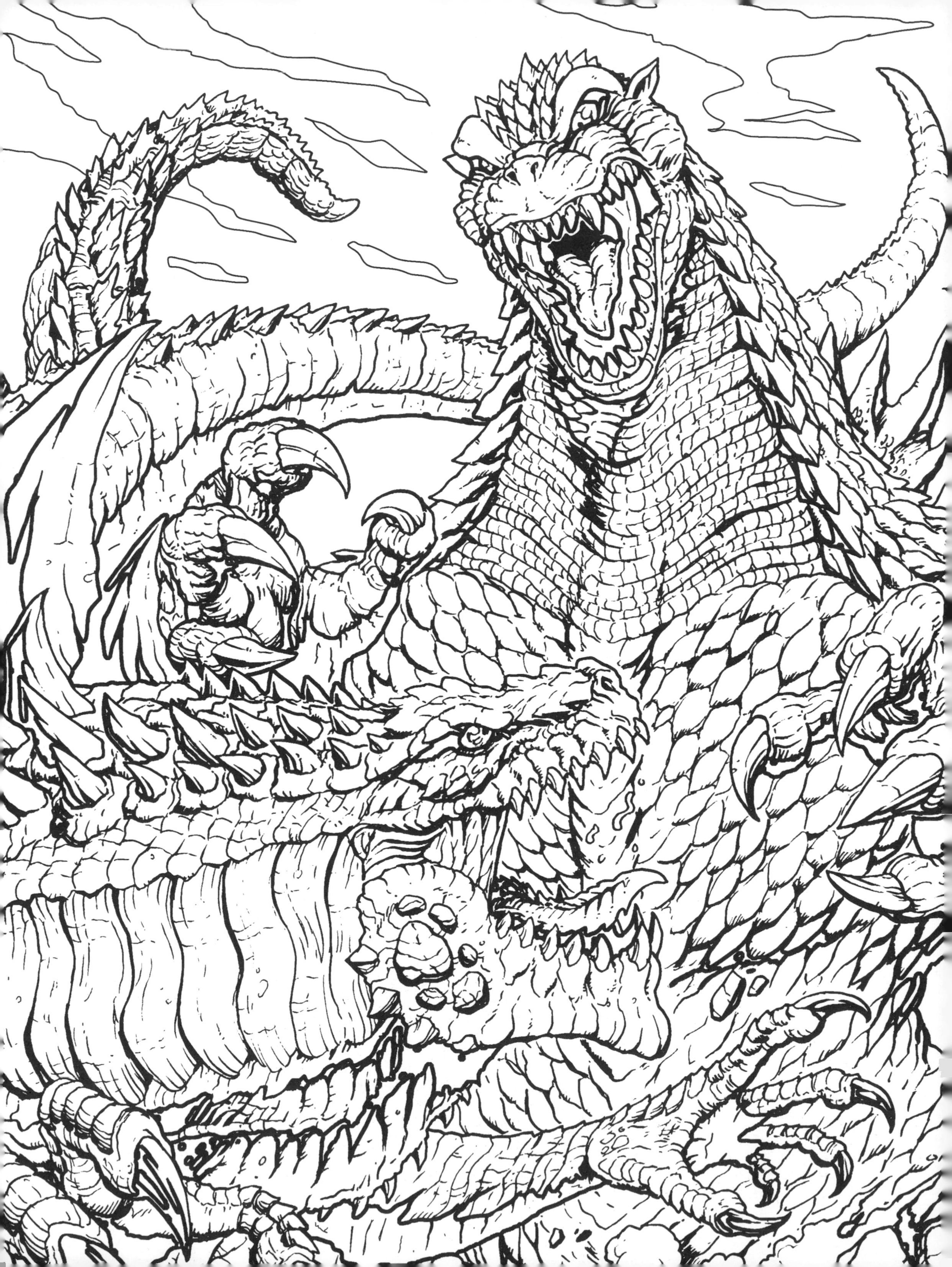

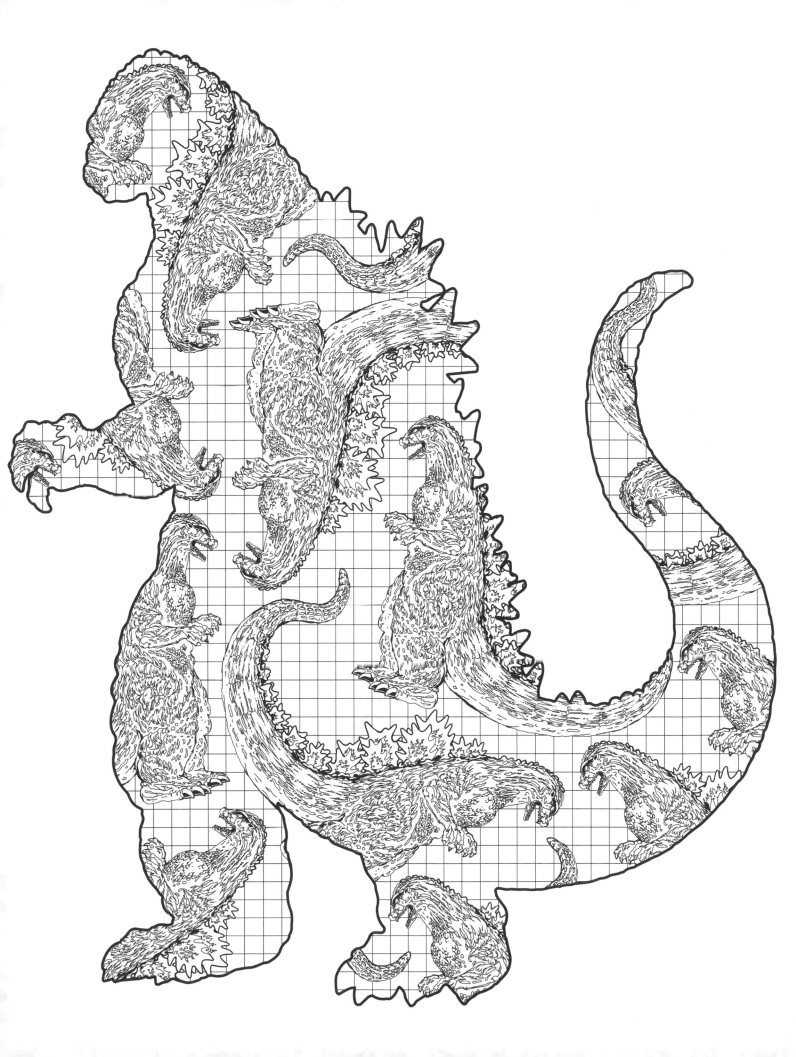

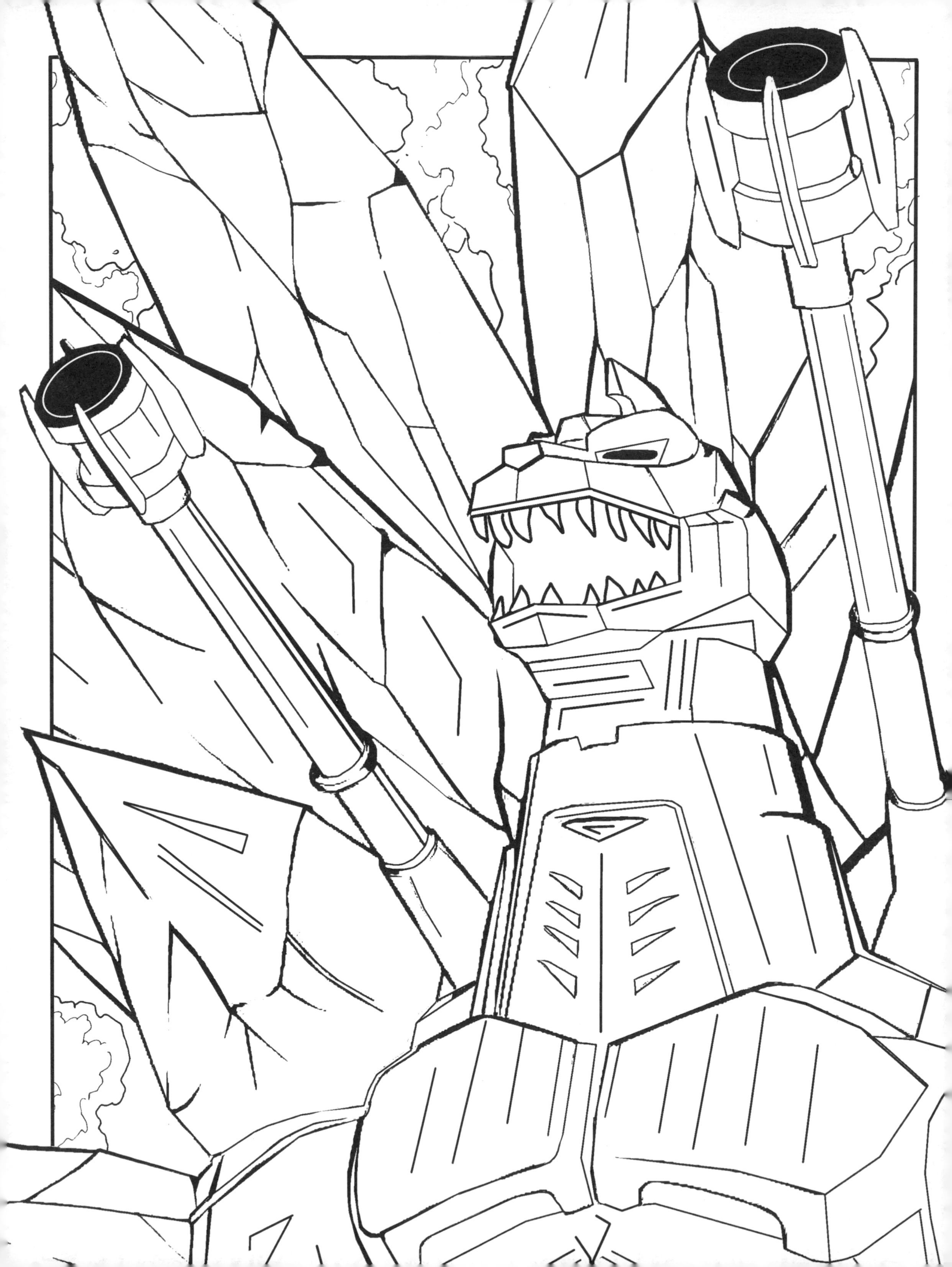

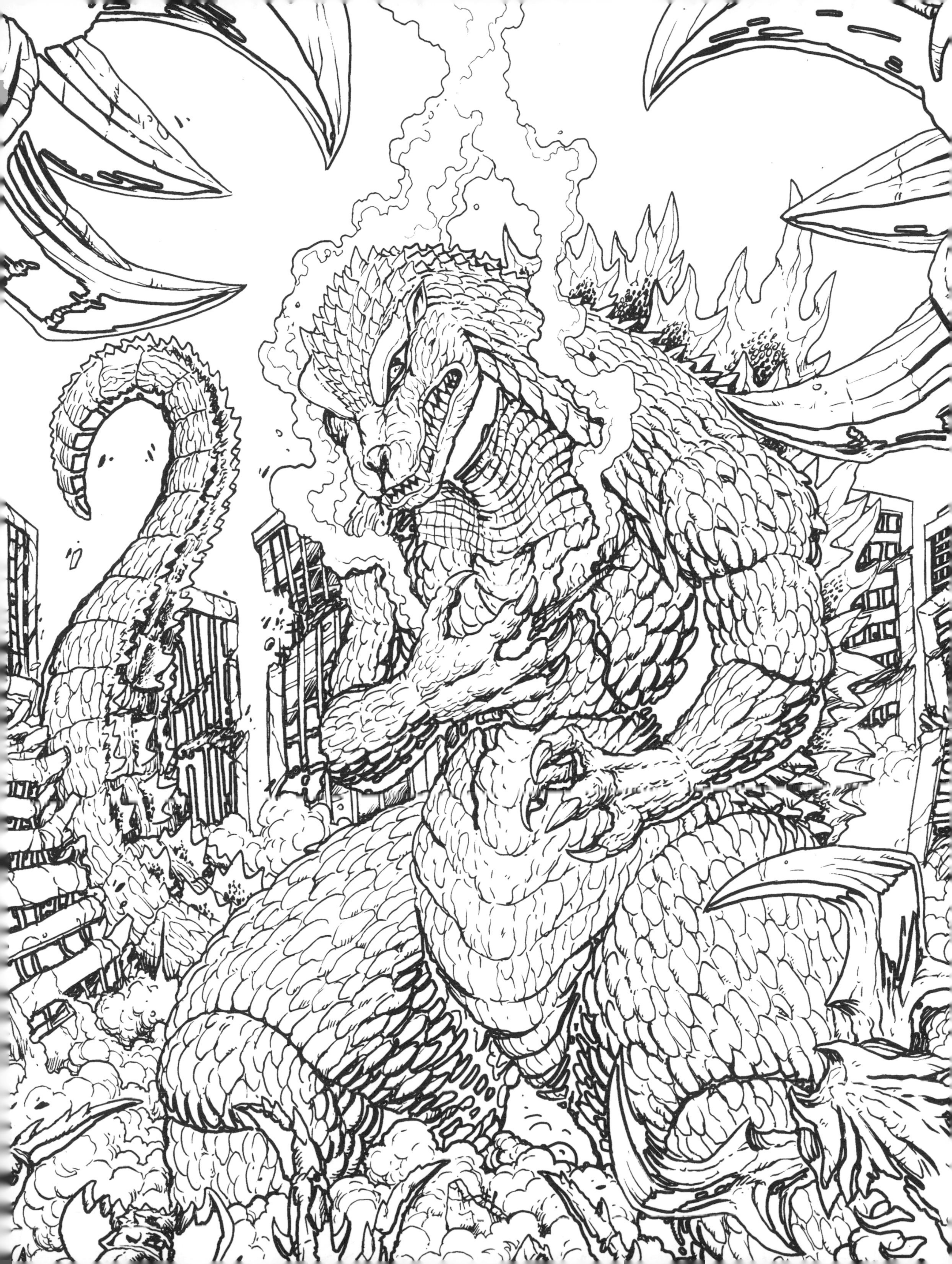

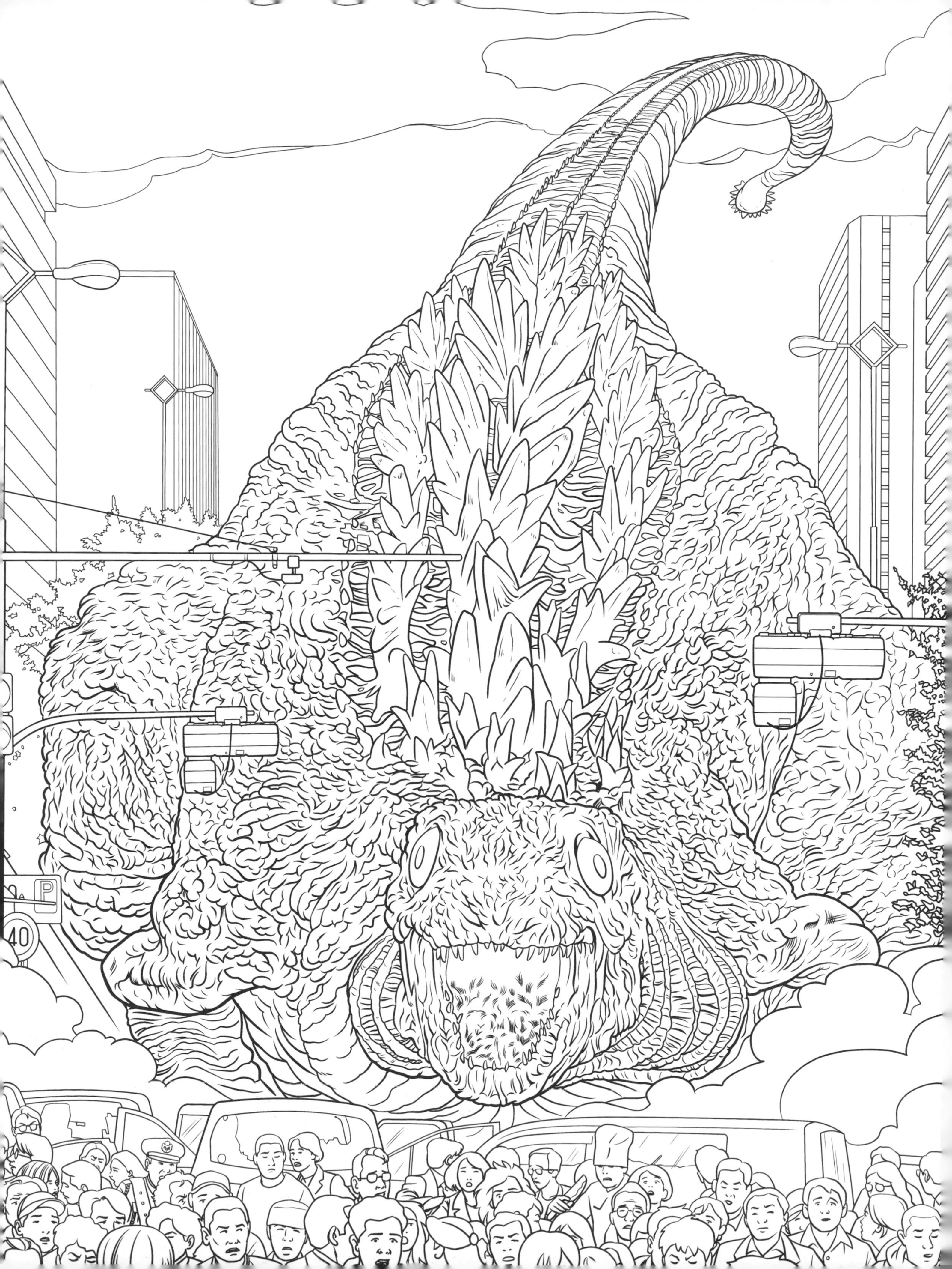
P
40

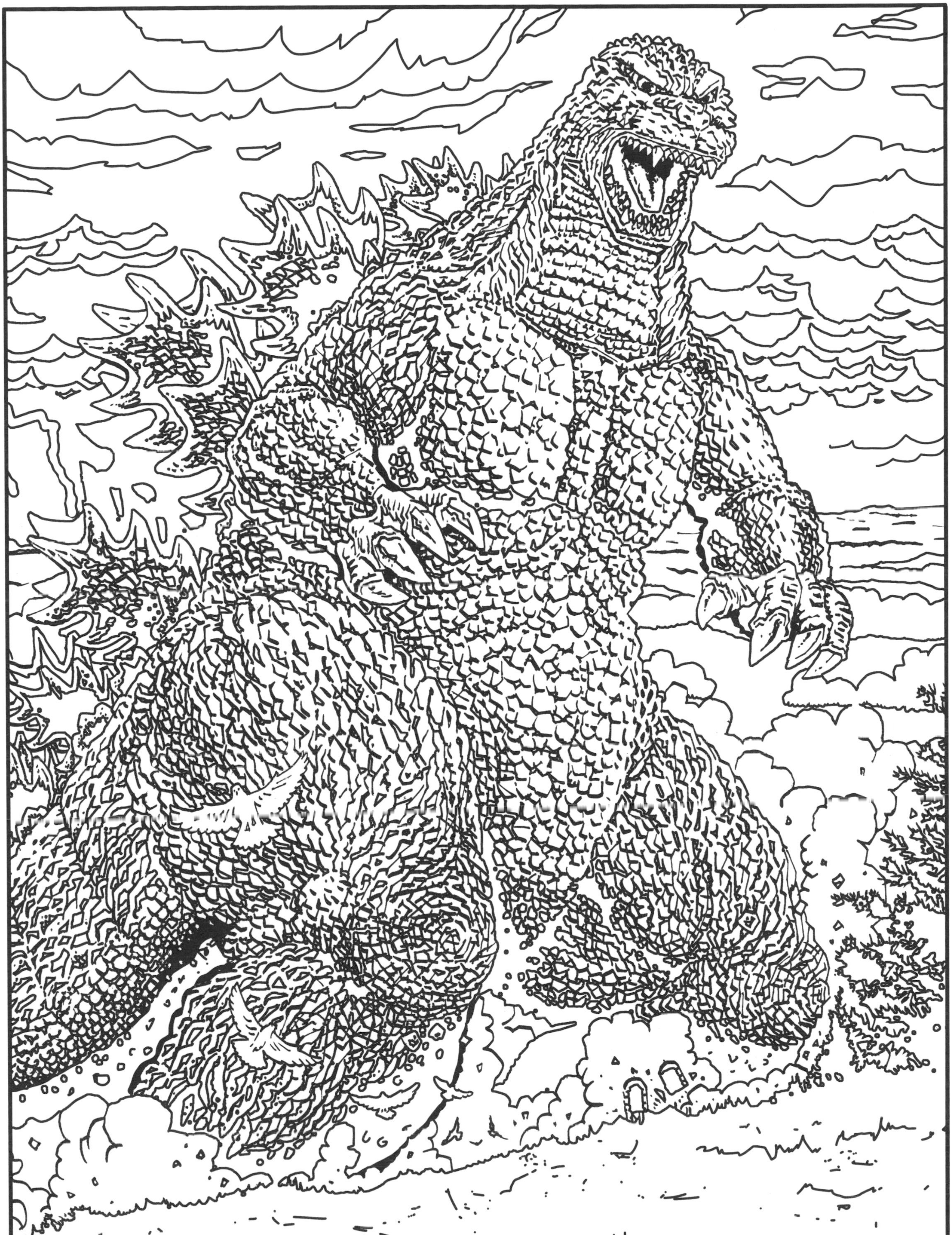

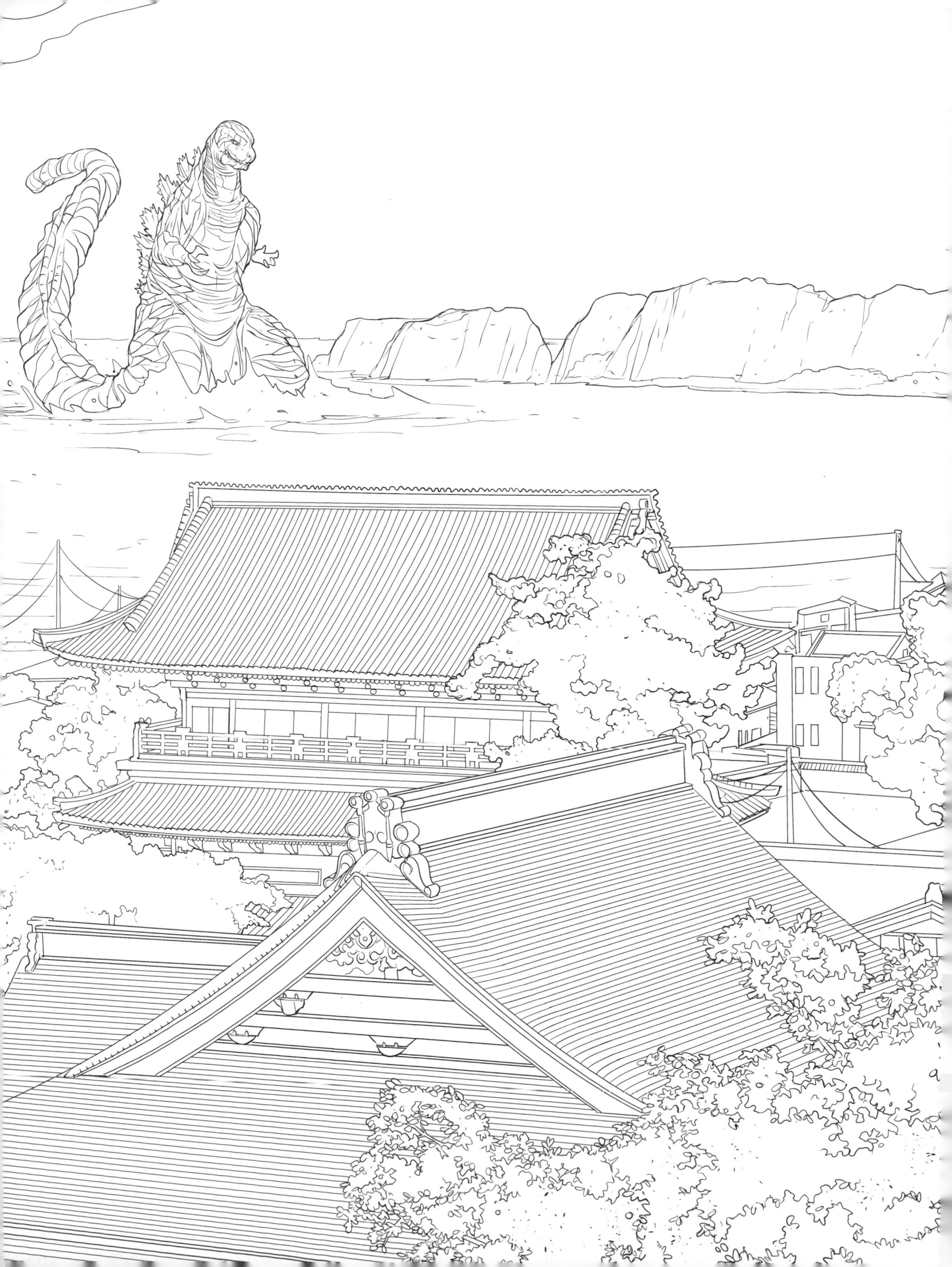

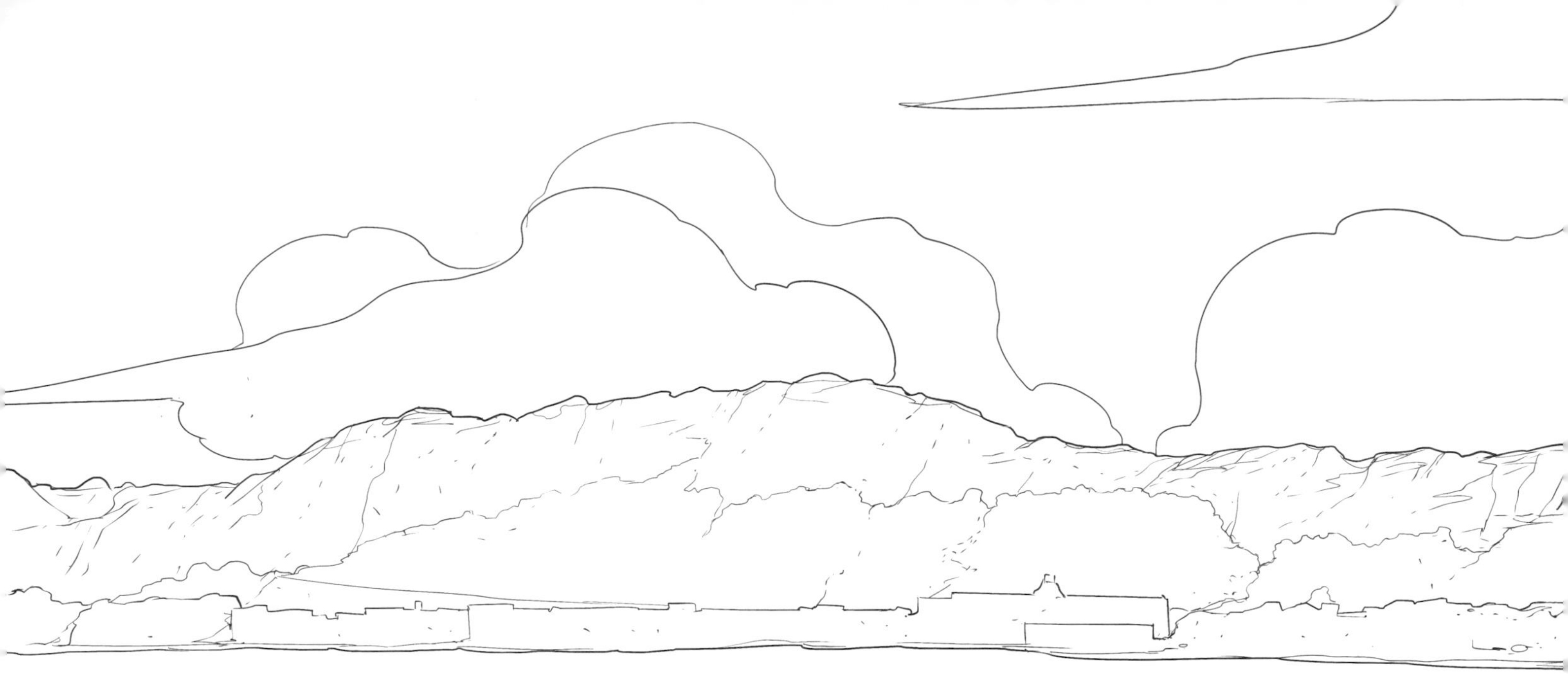

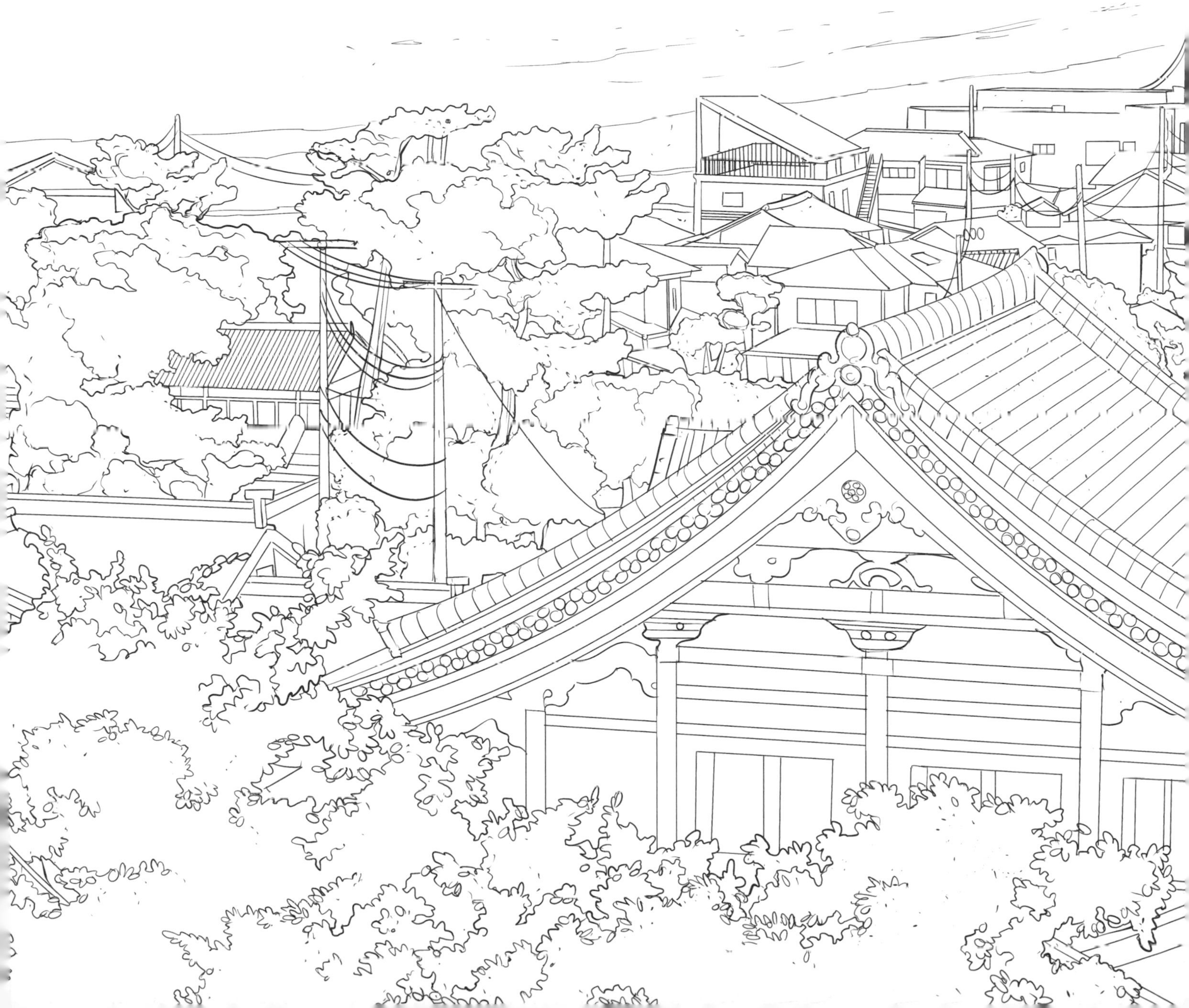

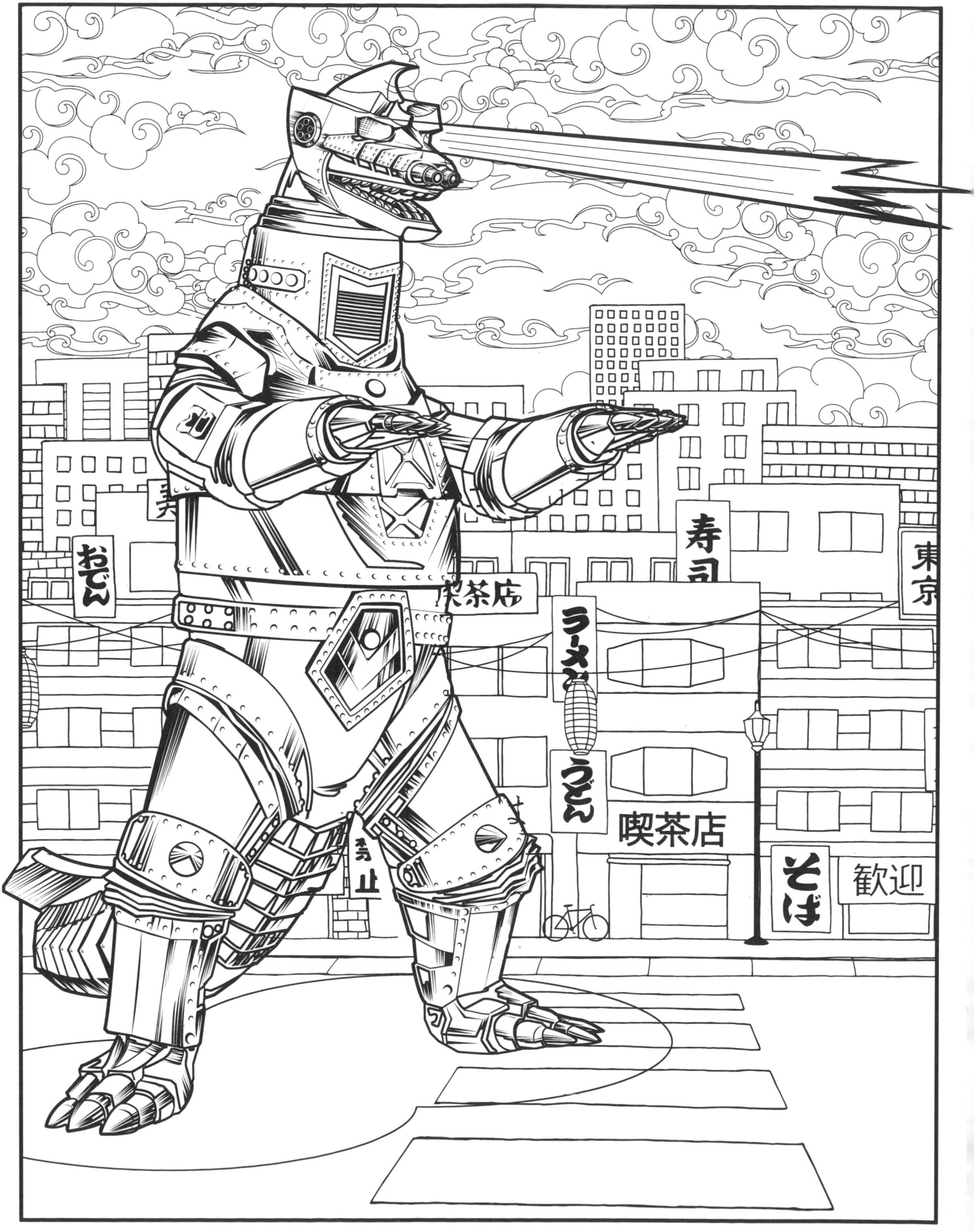
おでん
喫茶店
寿司
東京
うどん
喫茶店
そば
歓迎

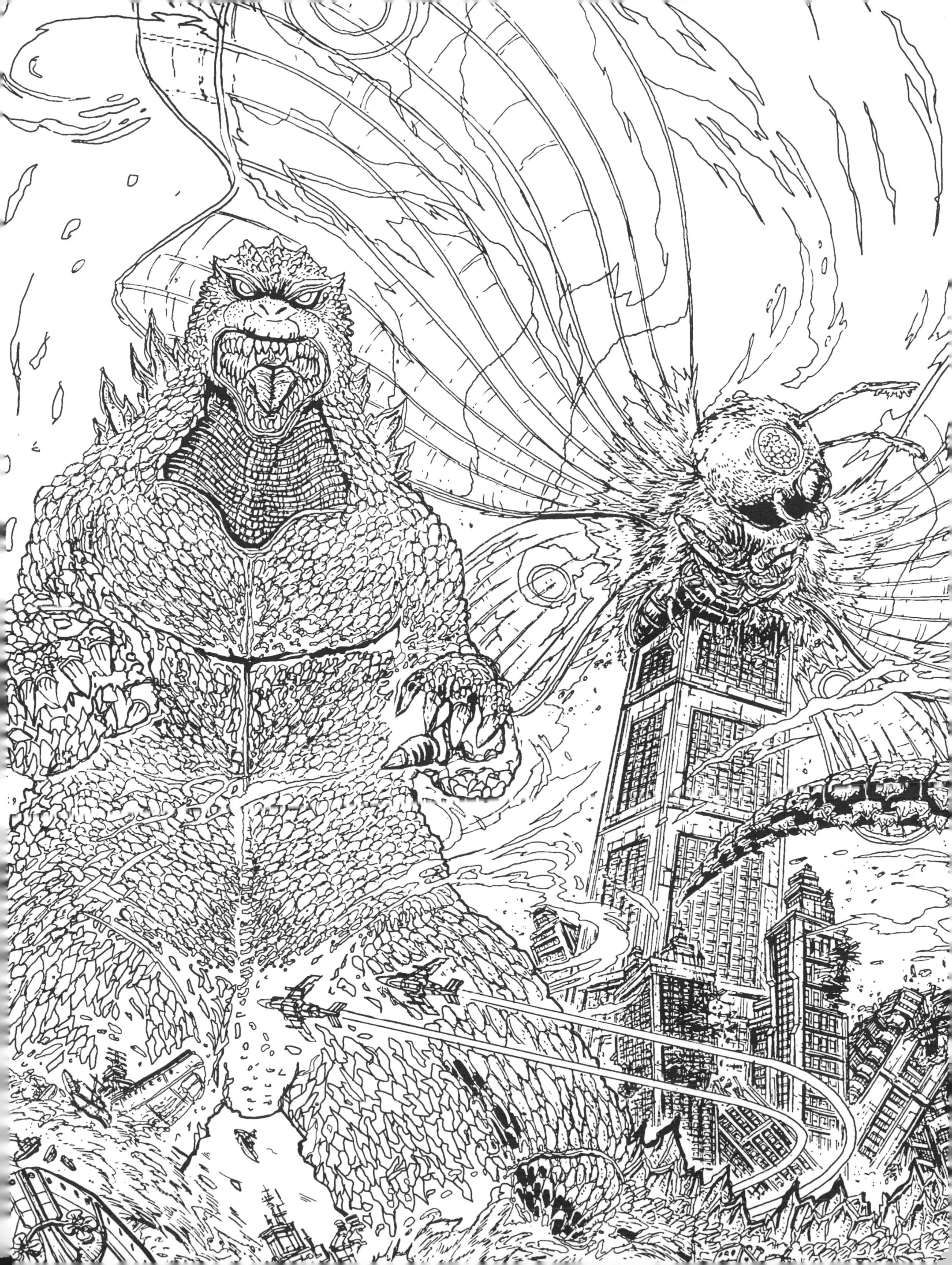

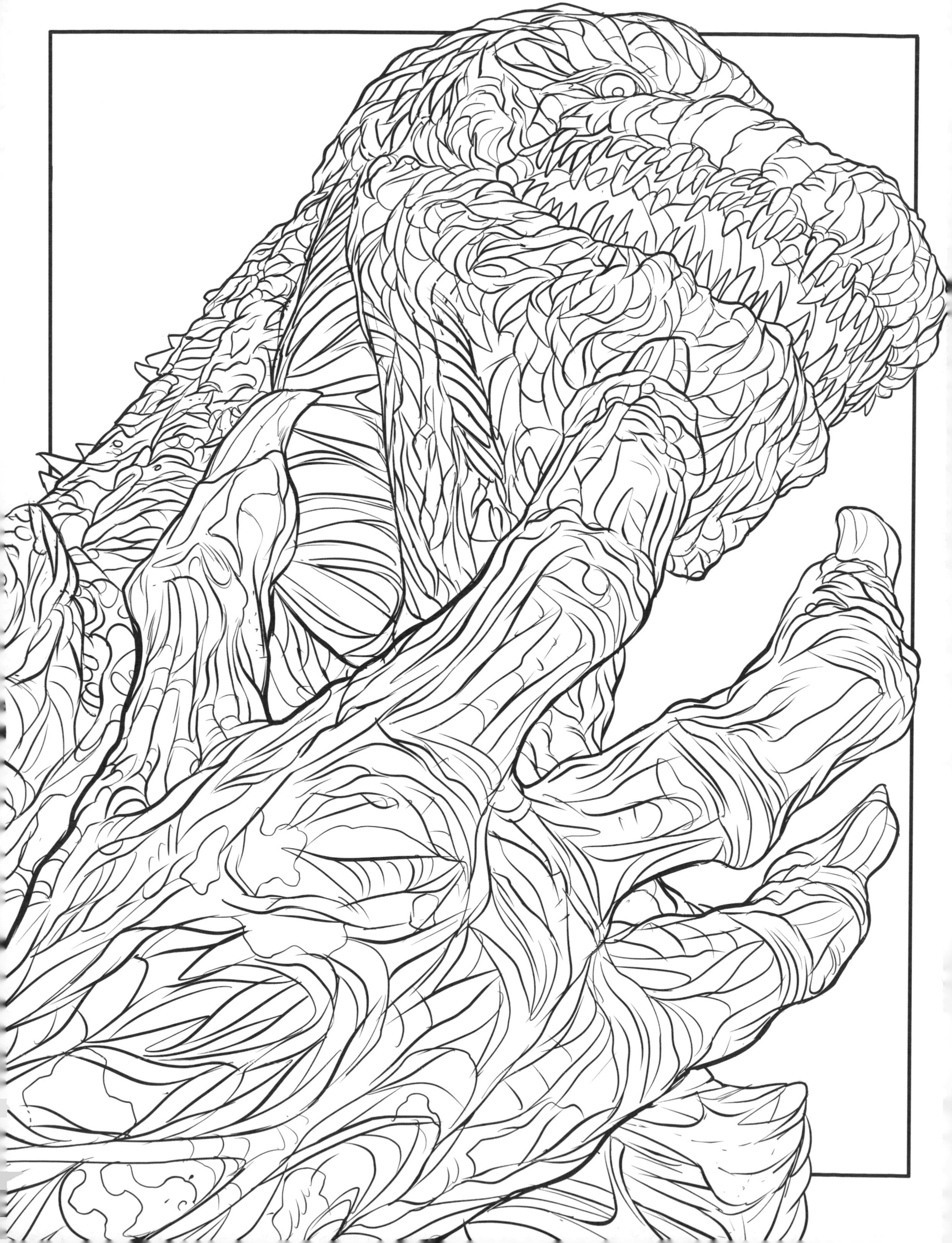

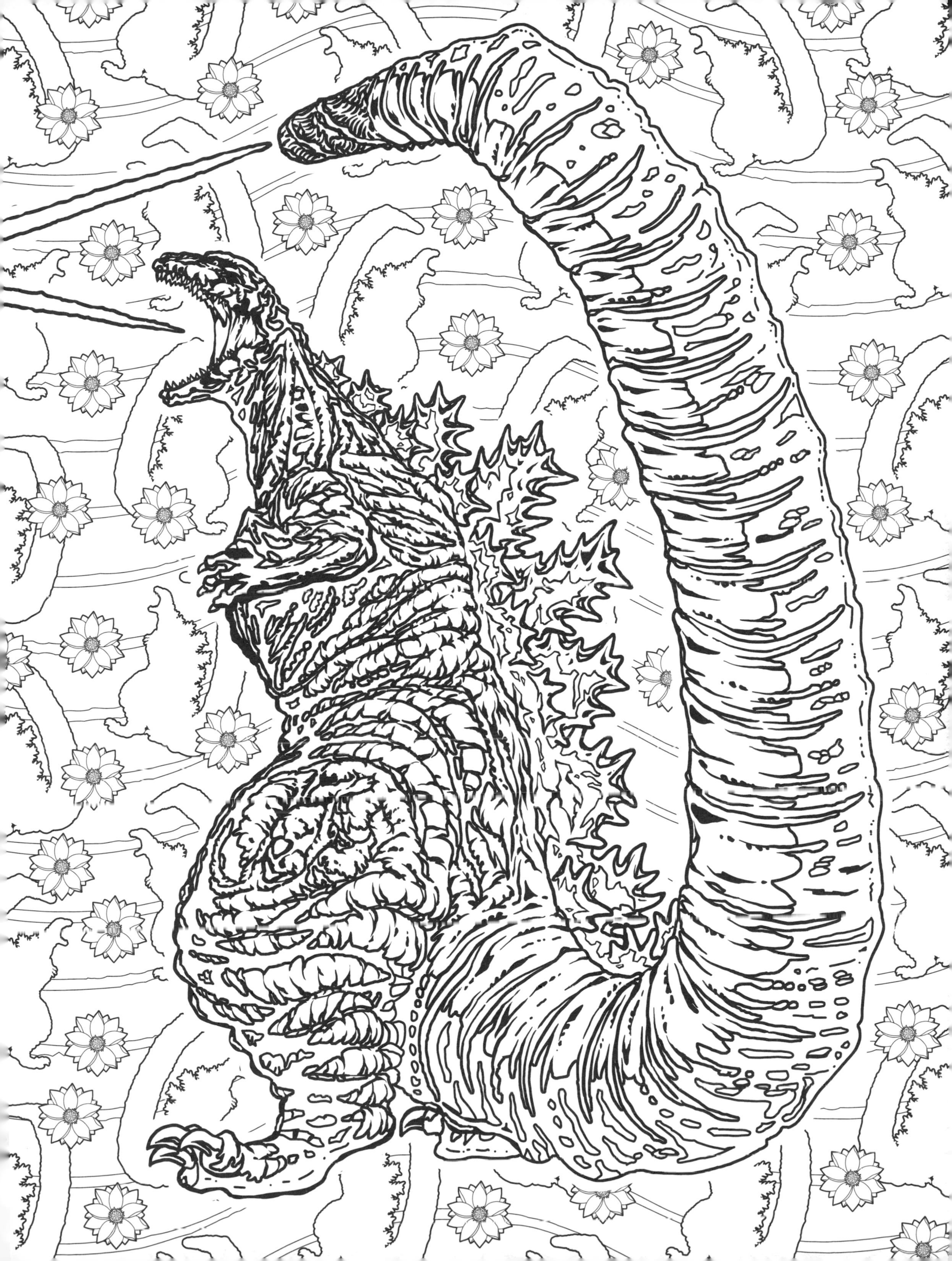

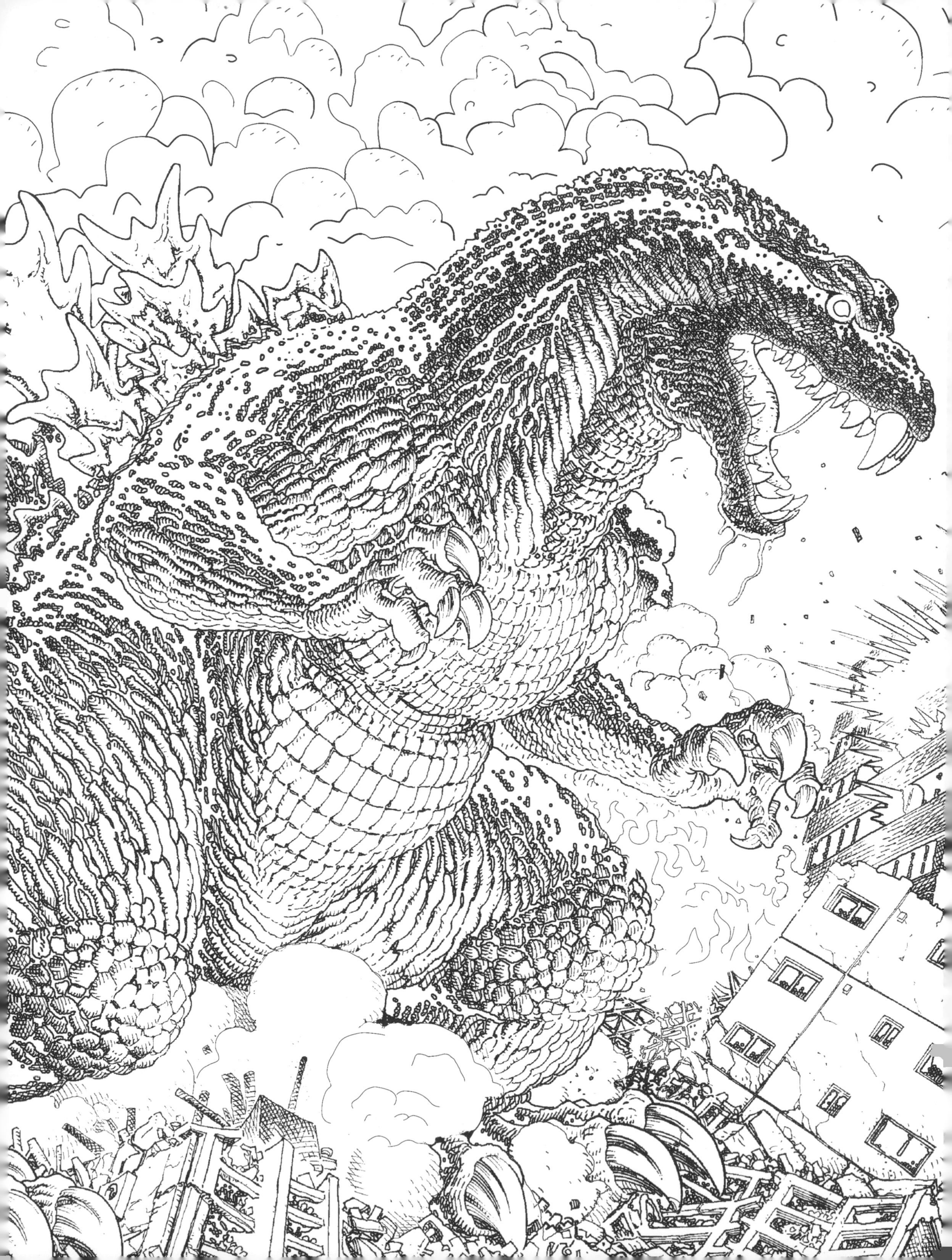